The
FINAL
COUNTDOWN

THE
FINAL
COUNTDOWN

The Seven Final Events
Before the Second Coming

BY
Clay McConkie, PhD

CFI
Springville, Utah

ISBN 13: 978-1-59955-017-6

Published by CFI, an imprint of Cedar Fort, Inc., 2373 W. 700 S., Springville, UT, 84663
Distributed by Cedar Fort, Inc. www.cedarfort.com

Library of Congress Cataloging-in-Publication Data

McConkie, Clay.
    The final countdown : the seven final events before the Second Coming / Clay McConkie.
        p. cm.
    Includes bibliographical references.
    ISBN 978-1-59955-017-6 (alk. paper)
    1. Second Advent. 2. Church of Jesus Christ of Latter-day Saints-- Doctrines. 3. Bible. N.T. Revelation--Criticism, interpretation, etc. I. Title.

BX8643.S43.M33 2007
236'.9--dc22

                    2007000592

Cover design by Nicole Williams
Cover design © 2007 by Lyle Mortimer
Edited and typeset by Lyndsee Simpson Cordes

Printed in the United States of America

1 0 9 8 7 6 5 4 3 2 1

Printed on acid-free paper

TABLE OF CONTENTS

With the advent of the year AD 2000, the announcement was made to the world that the two thousandth year since the birth of Jesus Christ, according to the current dating system, had begun. It was not the beginning of a new millennium at that time, as many people supposed, but rather the historic end of an old one.

Not until the year 2001 did the twenty-first century begin. Once again this was by way of the present calendar, a record of time that might be inaccurate by an undetermined number of years. There are those who believe that the birth of Christ, for example, occurred several years before the alleged calendar date, meaning that a year such as 2005 could actually turn out to be 2010 or later.

All of this can be a little confusing at times, but something that is nevertheless significant is that according to today's calendar, the year 2001 might also have been the beginning of the *seventh* millennium in the earth's total span of human history. This in turn suggests that the time of Adam and Eve dates back to the year 4000 BC. There is a problem here, however, since people often view the setting of the Garden of Eden much earlier in time than just six thousand years ago. In history books, civilizations are typically pictured as being well underway by that time period.

And yet the year 4000 BC still remains an interesting and unusual date, particularly in connection with the beginning of human history. It is also part of a very controversial subject. It was midway through the seventeenth century, in fact, that a man named James Ussher, an archbishop in the Anglican Church in Ireland, published his chronological calculations from the Bible, showing that the creation of the earth took place in 4004 BC. For more than two hundred years, his dating system in many instances was accepted by scholars and the public alike and was often used in the King James Version of the Bible in marginal dates and footnotes.

During the nineteenth century, however, the Ussher computations began to lose credibility for one reason or another, and today his chronology is generally not used. Dates too often do not synchronize with events in secular history, nor do they fit into the broad scheme of things chronologically. But his date of approximately 4000 BC for the beginning of human history is still interesting.

Such a date is also implied in the book of Revelation in the Bible where it talks about a book sealed on the backside with seven seals. As each seal is opened, certain things occur which purportedly refer to various divisions of the earth's human history.[1] The Bible does not say so specifically, but confirmation of this is found in a record of scripture known as the Doctrine and Covenants, which is endorsed by The Church of Jesus Christ of Latter-day Saints.

Referring to the seven seals, for example, this record states that "the first seal contains the things of the first thousand years, and the second also of the second thousand years, and so on until the seventh." The same record also says that the sealed book contained things pertaining to the earth "during the seven thousand years of its continuance, or its temporal existence."[2]

Certainly this is an interesting and important revelation. And in a day and age when the calculations of one such as

James Ussher are no longer accepted, and no consensus of opinion exists as to when human history on earth began, the information revealed in the Doctrine and Covenants is extremely noteworthy, even though the scripture is not widely regarded as authentic or canonical.

Not only is the information noteworthy, but it is also extraordinary in that it defines human existence on earth, including the years of the Millennium, as being seven thousand years in duration. In no other place in scripture or otherwise is there a more absolute statement. Without any qualification or reservation, the assertion in the Doctrine and Covenants is that when Adam and Eve partook of the forbidden fruit in the Garden of Eden, they became mortal and instigated a period of time that was to be a *temporal* existence of seven thousand years. Regardless of how such a declaration might compare with contemporary theories and philosophies in a modern-day society, the scripture nevertheless stands as it is written, and only time will tell whether or not it is a true prophecy. In the meantime, it exists with a host of other predictions and signs of the times, showing that the earth's population is definitely living in the last days and that the contemporary affairs of the world are rapidly drawing to a close. If the present calendar is anywhere near being accurate, and if the concept of seven thousand years is correct, world-culminating occurrences are already on the horizon.

As to the imminency of these events, however, much of it depends on the calendar, whether or not the world has actually passed into the twenty-first century. Whatever the correct date at present might be, it is probable that it is at least a few years later than the present calendar date if scholars are correct concerning the birth date of Jesus Christ.

It is also important to remember that even though a new century and millennium have allegedly begun, it does not mean that the Second Coming itself is imminent. The time of Christ's return, according to what he said during his ministry, is a date known only to his father. Whatever that date might be, the prediction is that it will not occur at the beginning of the new millennium. According to the Doctrine and Covenants once again, the time of Christ's second advent will be sometime "in the beginning of the seventh thousand years," the word *beginning* very possibly referring to an extensive period of time, even as much as the major part of the twenty-first century.

"We are to understand," the Doctrine and Covenants says, "that as God made the world in six days, and on the seventh day he finished his work, and sanctified it, and also formed man out of the dust of the earth, even so, in the beginning of the seventh thousand years will the Lord God sanctify the earth, and complete the salvation of man, and judge all things, and shall redeem all things, except that which he hath not put into his power, when he shall have sealed all things unto the end of all things; and the sounding of the trumpets of the seven angels [is] the preparing and finishing of his work, in the beginning of the seventh thousand years—the preparing of the way before the time of his coming."[3]

The sounding of the trumpets, therefore, spoken of in both the Doctrine and Covenants and the book of Revelation, will be a memorable occasion. This event will initiate the final preparations that need to be accomplished before the Second Coming. Certainly it is the signal that a final countdown is about to begin, one that will eventually reach a searing climax and bring current world history to an end.

And yet before all of this takes place, certain things need to occur, and the so-called seventh seal on the sealed book needs to be opened. There is also to be a one-half hour of silence in heaven, whatever that comes to mean, after which seven angels obtain their trumpets, and the last act in the earth's human history finally begins!

An important question pertaining to the book of Revelation concerns what was to happen during the time of the sixth seal and the sixth millennium, or in other words, the second thousand years after the time of Christ. The first four seals, sometimes identified as the four horses of the Apocalypse, are brief in their predictions and difficult to understand. These in turn are followed by the fifth seal that is a little more explanatory and refers to "the souls of them that were slain for the word of God."[4]

But beginning with the sixth seal, where considerably more information is given, there is an indication that certain events are out of order and that inaccuracies and inconsistencies exist. Indeed there is the suggestion of a serious problem and the possibility of translation or transmission errors in the formation of the Bible. Obviously this is a radical statement, but there is considerable evidence and proof for it.

Some of the predicted events, for example, and possibly most of them, seem to belong to a period of time well beyond that of the sixth seal or sixth millennium. The most notable of these are references to heaven opening like a scroll and mountains and islands moving out of their places. Especially in the scripture pertaining to heaven opening like a scroll, which refers to an event immediately prior to the Second Coming of

Christ when he appears in clouds of glory, there is the signal that this particular event does *not* belong to the sixth seal. The same might be true of the so-called movement of mountains and islands as well as possibly other events.

The events in question, as recorded in the book of Revelation, are as follows: "And I [John] beheld when he had opened the sixth seal, and, lo, there was a great earthquake; and the sun became black as sackcloth of hair, and the moon became as blood; and the stars of heaven fell unto the earth, even as a fig tree casteth her untimely figs, when she is shaken of a mighty wind. And the heaven [opened] as a scroll when it is rolled together; and every mountain and island [was] moved out of [its place]."[5]

Of course a lot depends on whether the time of the sixth seal has ended in regard to the present calendar. Even if the time of the seal has not ended, there is still a problem with the particular events relating to the scroll and the movement of mountains and islands, which probably need to be placed in time long after the opening of the seventh seal and very close to the Second Coming!

Once again the alleged misplacement of these two events alone strongly implies that there has been a translation or transmission problem in relation to the book of Revelation. In addition, the implication is that the events pertaining to the great earthquake and the phenomenon of sun, moon, and stars also belong to a later time. This in turn creates a void as well as a question as to what actually happened during the sixth seal. What other occurrences, in other words, are characteristic of this particular time period and at the same time fulfill religious prophecy?

A more likely occurrence of the actual conditions of the sixth seal, in fact, referring to the sixth thousand years of time, might more accurately be represented by the following: (1) widespread earthquakes, (2) wars and rumors of wars, (3) famines and pestilence, and (4) the preaching of the gospel throughout the world, all of which are cited in the twenty-fourth chapter of Matthew as being characteristic of the last days. Also, major events such as Genghis Khan's conquering of Asia and killing more than five million people, the bubonic plague in the fourteenth century taking another twenty-four million lives, and the regime of Nazi Germany executing six million Jews during World War II are all types of atrocity and pestilence that might represent things pertaining to the sixth seal. It is not difficult to find many events and circumstances that typify this period of time.

A tremendous amount of scholarship, in other words, might be unnecessary in focusing upon this problem. Instead it is a matter of acknowledging that events such as the folding scroll or moving mountains and islands definitely belong to a later time period and then attributing most or all of the scripture in Revelation 6:12–14 to the seventh seal rather than the sixth! At the same time, it suggests that the information in this particular area of the Bible is accurate and correct only if it has been translated correctly.

If this kind of situation is valid, it can be conjectured that the seventh seal has already been opened and that the seventh millennium has already begun. No one knows exactly, of course, but in viewing current history within the context and framework of the present calendar, it does not appear unlikely that the new millennium is already underway.

Although many views will undoubtedly differ with this type of statement, and recognizing that any number of things might have happened down through the centuries to affect the status of the present calendar, the following theoretical sequence of events and circumstances is a possibility. This will provide a tentative outline of what lies ahead. Seven of these events, beginning with the return of the lost tribes of Israel, are allegedly the ones that will immediately precede the Second Coming of Christ. And what is particularly interesting is that four of them, those shown in bold face print, pertain to the sixth seal in the book of Revelation!

1. The seventh seal is opened and the seventh millennium begins.
2. There is one-half hour of silence in heaven.
3. The seven angels are given trumpets (among other events).
4. Religious activity increases, including temple building, missionary work, and the continuation of the gathering of Israel.
5. A city and temple are constructed in Zion located in the central part of the United States.
6. The city and temple in Jerusalem are reconstructed.
7. A historic meeting takes place at Adam-ondi-Ahman.
8. Eventually the seven angels prepare to sound their trumpets.
9. The final plagues begin.
10. Seas and oceans go beyond their bounds.
11. The lost tribes of Israel return.
12. The Battle of Armageddon takes place.
13. **A gigantic earthquake** and other quakes occur, shaking the nations and breaking down the mountains.
14. Massive earthquakes continue, and the lands of Jerusalem and Zion are turned back into their own place as the earth is altered.
15. **The sun, moon, and stars phenomenon** occurs, and the sign of the Son of man appears.
16. The waters of the great deep are driven back into the north countries, reducing the sea level and **causing mountains and islands to move out of their places** and become one land.
17. **The curtain of heaven is unfolded,** and the face of the Lord is revealed.
18. The Second Coming and the first Resurrection come to pass.
19. A worldwide burning of the earth takes place.
20. The Millennium begins.

Such an outline of events is again theoretical, especially as far as sequence is concerned, but the main aspects of the earth's final countdown leading to the Second Coming are definitely in place. Indeed, it is possible that the seventh seal has been opened, or very soon will be, and the time is at hand for the predicted one-half hour of silence. Already the seven angels are waiting for their trumpets, and if these are the same angels who later will carry the vials containing the seven deadly plagues, or other angels like them, they will be assembling as a group and coming out one at a time from the temple which is in heaven!

A TIME OF SILENCE

The Bible briefly discusses what will happen when the final seal is first opened. "And when he had opened the seventh seal," the record says, "there was silence in heaven about the space of half an hour. And I saw the seven angels which stood before God; and to them were given seven trumpets."[6]

A continuing question pertains to the mysterious period of silence, a space of time calculated by some to be approximately twenty-one years by way of the formula in scripture that equates one thousand years on earth with one day of the Lord's time. Regardless of whether or not this is true, it is possible that the seventh seal has been opened, and that the world is already well into this so-called time of silence. If this is the case, what does this suggest for the near future?

Assuming hypothetically that the present-day calendar is generally correct, and making an adjustment to accommodate the idea that Jesus Christ might have been born a few years earlier than the traditional date, certainly it is possible to visualize that as much as ten years or more have passed since the beginning of the new millennium. Consequently, the time might rapidly be approaching when the Lord begins final preparations for his Second Coming. The predicted events that need to occur have definitely been narrowed down to only a few.

There is a timetable, however, and the signal for certain things to begin is when the angels in heaven start sounding their trumpets. "And the sounding of the trumpets of the seven angels," the scripture says, "[is] the preparing and finishing of his work, in the beginning of the seventh thousand years— the preparing of the way before the time of his coming."[7] According to the book of Revelation, this is also the general time period when seven angels carrying golden vials emerge from the temple and go forth upon the earth, pouring out the seven last plagues.

However, the drama of the angels with trumpets, as well as those with vials, will be preceded by still other important events, which may take place in the vicinity of the half hour of silence in heaven. Again the sequence is uncertain, but the events in question allegedly will occur *before* those in the last countdown, the space of time immediately preceding the Second Coming of Christ.

These preliminary events are only three in number, but they are monumental in importance, namely (1) the building of a large city and temple called Zion in the central part of the United States, (2) the reconstruction of the city and temple in Jerusalem, and (3) a historic meeting scheduled to take place at a site in America called Adam-ondi-Ahman. Without question, the magnitude and significance of these three events, all occurring in modern-day society, are almost beyond comprehension, and all three of them, according to religious prophecy, must happen before the time of the last countdown and the Second Coming!

In regard to the mysterious time of silence, it could be that to some extent, it is an interim or introduction for these particular events. It could also be a symbolic time in heaven when the angels receive their final instructions and prepare to sound their trumpets. It might be a grand preliminary, in other words, to "the preparing and finishing" of the Lord's work. Whatever the situation might be, it will be a strategic point in human history when some significant events are taking place.

The city and temple to be built in America are particularly interesting. As a kind of namesake of the ancient temple that used to be in Jerusalem on the opposite side of the globe, the new temple will represent Christianity in the New World as contrasted with that in the Old World. The city of Zion, in which the temple is to be erected, is reminiscent of the Holy City in Palestine and will be the scene of many important events during the last days, including the historic arrival of people coming from the north countries who are descendants of the ten lost tribes of Israel!

Indeed, the American city, sometimes referred to as the New Jerusalem, will eventually become one of two world capitals, one in the United States and the other in Jerusalem. The ancient prophecy will then be fulfilled which says that "out of Zion shall go forth the law, and the word of the Lord from Jerusalem."[8]

As to the building of the temple in what has been called the "center place of Zion," the project will be a continuation of a vast program of temple construction already in progress, albeit on a much larger scale. The temple in Zion, in fact, will not be just one building but twenty-four, according to the original plan, a combination of individual temples occupying two enlarged city blocks fifteen acres each.

These twenty-four temples have also been described as rooms or compartments all joined together in a circular form and arched over the center.[9] But the idea in the beginning appears rather to have been separate structures. According to a plan submitted by Joseph Smith of The Church of Jesus Christ of Latter-day Saints, who was the original designer and architect of the temple complex, there were to be twelve temples on each block, situated alternately in rows of three. The first of these buildings, being eighty-seven feet long and sixty-one feet wide, was to be built near the center of the first block.

In any case, the preliminary plan has been in existence for well over one hundred and fifty years, and when the time comes for its implementation, or one similar to it, the actual construction of the temple complex and the central portion of the city of Zion and its environs could occur very quickly.

What is important in all of this, of course, is that this particular temple, the construction of which will be a tremendous undertaking, is scheduled to take place *before* the time of the Second Coming. This is implied in a statement made by Joseph Smith in which he said that a temple of similar standing would definitely be built in Jerusalem during this time period.

"Judah must return," he said, referring to the gathering of the Jewish people in modern-day Palestine. "Jerusalem must be rebuilt, and the temple, and water come out from under the temple . . . and all this must be done before the Son of Man will make His appearance."[10] The idea is that both temples, the one in Palestine and the other in America, will be in place at the time of Christ's return.

There are other indications that the temple in Zion will be in existence at this time, but the fact that one will be in Jerusalem is reason to think that a temple will also exist in the New Jerusalem located in the United States. This is suggested in the Doctrine and Covenants where it refers to the temple in Zion, saying that it is a building that "shall be reared in this generation."[11] The statement is dated 1832, and although references to generations are sometimes ambiguous, still it is very possible that a large temple complex will be built in Zion by the time of the Second Coming.

In addition, there are scriptures pertaining to this period which refer to Jesus standing "upon Mount Zion,"[12] meaning the New Jerusalem, and "upon the Land of Zion."[13] Another scripture tells about the returning ten tribes visiting Zion and being "crowned with glory."[14] Again, all of these are implications that there will be a completed temple in America, along with the one in Jerusalem, before the Second Coming of Christ. Certainly it will be at these two locations that some of the most outstanding events will occur!

One of these events, which turns out to be quite surprising, is the resumption and continuation for a time of the offering of animal sacrifices. A religious practice which has been dormant in Christianity for centuries will be temporarily reintroduced as part of a "restitution of all things" during an era in the latter days that has been termed scripturally as the dispensation of the fulness of times. Specifically, it involves the idea that as part of a restitution or restoration, it will be the purpose of the Lord "that in the dispensation of the fulness of times he might gather together in one all things in Christ, both which are in heaven, and which are on earth."[15]

All of the principles and ordinances of the gospel that were introduced and practiced during former dispensations, those relating to Adam, Enoch, Noah, Abraham, Moses, and Jesus Christ, will be restored during a seventh and final dispensation and practiced as part of a preparation for the Second Coming and the beginning of the Millennium. All basic aspects of true religion, including animal sacrifice, will be reintroduced, or introduced for the first time, during a grand program of restoration.

When the huge temple complex is constructed in the central portion of the United States, accompanying the building of the city of Zion or New Jerusalem, many important events again will be taking place. And since these will all happen prior to the Lord's second advent, when they do occur, people will know that concluding events are imminent and that the time of his coming is near!

In regard to animal sacrifice, the reintroduction of this ancient practice will be a significant event. Certainly it involves a concept not always easy to understand, particularly in the context of modern society, and yet it is a concept that was comprehended fully by Joseph Smith, the man associated with the Doctrine and Covenants and the main figure in the process of restitution and restoration.

"The offering of sacrifice," he said on one occasion, "has ever been connected and forms a part of the duties of the Priesthood. It began with the Priesthood, and will be continued until after the coming of Christ, from generation to generation . . . These sacrifices, as well as every ordinance belonging to the Priesthood, will, when the Temple of the Lord shall be built, and the sons of Levi be purified, be fully restored and attended to in all their powers, ramifications, and blessings. This ever did and ever will exist when the powers of the Melchizedek Priesthood are sufficiently manifest; else how can the restitution of all things spoken of by the holy Prophets be brought to pass?"[16]

While it is true that the law of Moses was fulfilled at the time that Jesus finished his ministry, at which time the law came to an end, Joseph Smith in his comments on animal sacrifice was quick to point out that the fulfillment and conclusion of the law itself did not preclude further animal sacrifices sometime in the future. "It is not to be understood," he said, "that the law of Moses will be established again with all its rites and varieties of ceremonies: this has never been spoken of by the prophets; but those things which existed prior to Moses' day, namely, sacrifice, will be continued."[16]

Another thing he emphasized was that animal sacrifice, after it has been restored, will definitely be practiced until the Second Coming of Christ. During the intervening period, it will continue "from generation to generation." For whatever reason, this ancient principle will be extended for an indefinite period of time "with all its authority, power, and blessings." Again, all of this is not only interesting, but it confirms the existence of a temple in the city of Zion or New Jerusalem prior to the Millennium and is also one of the major signs of the times in the final stages of the latter days!

Another event of great importance, along with the building of the temple in the United States, will be the reconstruction of the ancient temple in Jerusalem. Among all of the signs that have been given, this is one of the most significant, yet possibly one of the most difficult to fulfill as far as human participation is concerned. But it is an event that needs to take place, according to religious prophecy, and it needs to occur *before* the time of the of the Second Coming.

During ancient times, there were three different temples in Jerusalem, all existing in separate time periods but at the same location. David would have liked to build a temple, but because he was a man of war, it was his son Solomon who eventually ended up constructing it. Traditionally, it was located at the same place in the land of Moriah where Abraham went to sacrifice his son Isaac. On the same hilltop where a sacrifice almost took place that day, but was stopped by an angel, Solomon built one of the most splendid structures in the ancient world.

After the temple was destroyed several centuries later, and following the Babylonian captivity, it was rebuilt on the same site by Zerubbabel and his associates. The building continued in existence for approximately five hundred years, going through many different stages and desecrations. Finally, a short time before the birth of Christ, Herod the Great began making changes and improvements, enlarging and refurbishing the previous structure at an enormous financial cost and turning it into something far beyond anything anyone had previously known. Though Herod himself was a despicable ruler, Jesus, during his earthly ministry, accepted the new temple as his own, referring to it on one occasion as his father's house.

Three different temples, therefore, once existed at the location in Jerusalem regarded today as the Temple Mount. All three have since been destroyed, but in their place is a memory held by millions of people throughout the world, belonging to the religions of Islam, Judaism, and Christianity. They all look upon the Holy City as part of their religious heritage. Certain members of two of these groups, in fact, say that someday they want to independently rebuild the ancient temple. Both The Church of Jesus Christ of Latter-day Saints and a Jewish organization called the Temple Institute, possibly among others, look upon this as an important undertaking and a specific goal for the future.

However, Jews or Christians trying to build a temple on the Temple Mount would pose a real problem. In the mind of Islam, this particular location is the third most important religious site in the world, the other two being Mecca and Medina. Anyone threatening or disrupting the status of the Dome of the Rock or the nearby al-Aqsa Mosque, both situated on the Temple Mount, would be tantamount to open warfare, a potentiality that already exists between the Israelis and Palestinians.

Still the most logical and meaningful area in which to build the temple, at least as far as Judaism is concerned, is the present-day Temple Mount, on the exact site of the original building. The group known as the Temple Institute, for example, has stated that its "ultimate goal is to see Israel rebuild the Holy Temple on Mount Moriah in Jerusalem, in accord with the Biblical commandments."[17] This means that if the belief turns out to be correct that the hill known as

Moriah in the book of Genesis is the same location where Solomon, Zerubbabel, and Herod constructed their temples, the Temple Mount is definitely a logical place.

It is interesting to note that the Temple Institute is preparing vessels and equipment in Jerusalem to be used in contructing a future temple. "These vessels and priestly garments are being fashioned today according to the exact biblical requirements," they say, "specifically for use in the future Holy Temple." The group considers it important to inform people about the "significance of Mount Moriah, the Temple Mount in Jerusalem, the only site in the world that is considered holy by the Jewish people, and the only site in the world which [God] chose to rest his presence through the establishment of the Holy Temple."[17]

Of course much of this is related to current world problems and the complex political situation. Certainly whether or not anyone rebuilds an ancient temple in the modern city of Jerusalem remains to be seen. But at least the prospects of someone doing it are there, and more than one organization evidently has it in mind.

In 1990, one of these groups, the Temple Mount Faithful, reportedly issued leaflets calling for a mass Jewish pilgrimage to the Temple Mount on one of the Jewish holidays. The Palestinians immediately became concerned that the group might be planning to lay a cornerstone for a future temple that would replace Islamic holy sites, particularly the Dome of the Rock and the al-Aqsa Mosque. In October of that year, an incident occurred that resulted in twenty-two people being killed and more than 150 wounded, according to news reports. All of them were Palestinians. Those involved were among those responding to a call from Muslim religious leaders to help protect Palestinian interests on the Temple Mount. It was an unfortunate occurrence, undoubtedly reflecting others which might have taken place earlier or would occur later.

But in regard to the organization known as the Temple Institute, there definitely might be a problem constructing a building on Mount Moriah, the present location of the Dome of the Rock. If the institute insists that the new temple be located on the spot where the original temple stood, for example, this supposedly would conflict with Islam's sacred dome, which they say marks the place where Abraham took Isaac for sacrifice.

Yet if the theory of a professor associated with the Hebrew University in Jerusalem, Asher Kaufman, is correct, the location of the earlier temple was not on the site of the Dome of the Rock, as commonly believed, but some twenty-six meters or eighty-five feet to the north.[18] This would allow a new temple to be built on the exact location as the original by either Jews or Christians without seriously disrupting any religious worship of the Muslims. Even if all of these calculations should prove to be incorrect, a fourth temple, following those of Solomon, Zerurabbel, and Herod, could ultimately be built at some other place in the city.

The Church of Jesus Christ of Latter-day Saints, another group interested in rebuilding the Jerusalem temple and most of whose members claim to be descended from the ancient tribe of Ephraim, in contrast with the Jewish people who claim a descent from Judah, could possibly end up building a temple on a site such as the nearby Mount of Olives. The Church has already erected an imposing building in that area for educational purposes, and it is not unlikely that someday it could also rebuild an ancient temple there.

But wherever such a temple is constructed, and whoever it is that builds it, the event will be fraught with unusual meaning and significance. Not only will it be a memorable religious occurrence in and of itself, but it will also be an important sign of the times. Again, Joseph Smith stated that it would be one of the events taking place prior to the Second Coming.

"Judah must return," he said. "Jerusalem must be rebuilt, and the temple, and water come out from under the temple . . . and all this must be done before the Son of Man will make His appearance."[19]

It is also interesting to note that something very unusual will happen after the temple is built, an event no less significant than the temple itself. Water will emerge from under the temple and, according to Old Testament scriptures, will result in a miraculous transformation in the adjacent desert and countryside to the east. Whereas the Dead Sea is among the saltiest bodies of water in the world, of which twenty-five percent or more is mineral salts, the time will come according to prophecy when waters coming out from the temple will flow into this inland sea and "heal" its waters, after which fish will abound, and the rivers carrying incoming water will be lined with trees.

One of the prophets who referred to this remarkable event was Ezekiel, who in talking about the temple said that "waters issued out from under the threshold of the house eastward . . . and go down into the desert and go into the sea: which being brought forth into the sea, the waters shall be healed.

"And it shall come to pass," he continued, "that everything that liveth, which moveth, whithersoever the rivers shall come, shall live: and there shall be a very great multitude of fish, because these waters shall come thither: for they shall be healed; and every thing shall live whither the river cometh."[20]

The prophet Joel also talked briefly about this event, saying, "All the rivers of Judah shall flow with waters, and a fountain shall come forth of the house of the Lord, and shall water the valley of Shittim."[21] Still another prophet, Zechariah, stated that it is "in that day, that living waters shall go out from Jerusalem; half of them toward the former sea, and half of them toward the hinder sea: in summer and in winter shall it be."[22]

Two latter-day temples, therefore, one in Jerusalem and the other in the central part of the United States, are scheduled to be built before the Second Coming of Jesus Christ. These will allegedly be similar to temples such as those now being constructed by The Church of Jesus Christ of Latter-day Saints in many places throughout the world, but they will be at a different level and with a different status. Although their main purpose will be to provide religious ordinances and instruction, they will also be in connection with two world capitals of the future, one in Jerusalem and the other in the American city of Zion. Indeed, these will be historic buildings, and when their construction begins, people will know that the Second Coming is truly imminent!

Sometime before the Lord comes a second time, according to religious prophecy, prior to the "clouds of heaven" incident referred to in the Bible and the beginning of the Millennium, he will make an appearance at a place called Adam-ondi-Ahman, a locality unknown to most people in today's society but one of tremendous importance nevertheless. In a quiet valley in northwestern Missouri, a secluded place where no one would suspect that an event of great meaning and import will take place, he is scheduled to make a historic visit. It will bear the name of another visit that is said to have occurred in this same vicinity more than 5,000 years ago.

"Three years previous to the death of Adam," as stated in the Doctrine and Covenants, "he (Adam) called Seth, Enos, Cainan, Mahalaleel, Jared, Enoch, and Methuselah, who were all high priests, with the residue of his posterity who were righteous, into the valley of Adam-ondi-Ahman, and there bestowed upon them his last blessing. And the Lord appeared unto them, and they rose up and blessed Adam, and called him Michael, the prince, the archangel.

"And the Lord administered comfort unto Adam, and said unto him: I have set thee to be at the head; a multitude of nations shall come of thee, and thou art a prince over them forever. And Adam stood up in the midst of the congregation;

and notwithstanding he was bowed down with age, being full of the Holy Ghost, predicted whatsoever should befall his posterity unto the latest generation."[23]

This was certainly a momentous occasion, and it took place somewhere outside the Garden of Eden almost 1,000 years after Adam and Eve had been cast out because of disobedience. The event allegedly did not occur in the Old World, as most people believe, but rather in the New World. The belief and concept expounded in the Doctrine and Covenants, for example, is that the site of the garden mentioned in the book of Genesis was in present-day North America and not on the other side of the globe in Mesopotamia or some other locale. Among other things, this means that the ark during the great flood in Noah's time, after leaving the original area and sailing half way around the world, ended up on Mount Ararat in what is now eastern Turkey.

A very important idea that modern scripture has revealed, however, is that the Garden of Eden was not only in North America but specifically in the central part of the United States in what is now northwestern Missouri. To many people, this will be an astonishing and remarkable statement, but such is nevertheless the case. An exact reference to it is found in the Doctrine and Covenants where, in talking about the place called Adam-ondi-Ahman in Missouri, it says that it was "the land where Adam dwelt."[24] In the same area of scripture, it states that this is also the place that Christ will visit during an important meeting that will occur prior to the Second Coming.

Again, all of this is information contained in one particular scriptural record. Along with additional information found in the Bible, this record describes events in historic meetings yet to come. In the book of Daniel, for example, a vision is described that the prophet had at one time, telling about someone referred to as the Ancient of days, who was Adam, who came for the purpose of reviewing and judging the people. Undoubtedly, this was a future occurrence, yet how much of it pertains to what will occur at Adam-ondi-Ahman is unclear. In any case, the principal figure involved is Adam.

"I beheld till the thrones were cast down," the record says, "and the Ancient of days did sit, whose garment was white as snow, and the hair of his head like the pure wool: his throne was like the fiery flame, and his wheels as burning fire. A fiery stream issued and came forth from before him: thousand thousands ministered unto him, and ten thousand times ten thousand stood before him: the judgment was set, and the books were opened."[25]

In this dream, after witnessing four beasts appear one after the other, Daniel beheld the vision of Adam appearing in white with the bearing and majesty of a prince or king. Throngs of people attended him and stood before him, numbering in the millions, according to the dream's description, even to the extent of one hundred million. At that time, the books were opened, and Adam assumed his position before the people as a magistrate and judge.

The next section of the dream, however, suddenly presents a very different scene and situation. "I saw in the night visions," Daniel related, "and, behold, one like the Son of man came with the clouds of heaven, and came to the Ancient of days, and they brought him near before him. And there was given him dominion, and glory, and a kingdom, that all people, nations, and languages, should serve him: his dominion is an everlasting dominion, which shall not pass away, and his kingdom that which shall not be destroyed."[26]

Definitely at this point in Daniel's dream, there would appear to be a division into two separate occurrences or situations, one pertaining to Adam in a judicial capacity, the other where he is visited by the Son of man, meaning Jesus Christ. In one there are countless millions of people involved, whereas in the other, especially if the situation is to be equated with the meeting at Adam-ondi-Ahman, there is a much smaller number.

When Joseph Smith commented upon this second situation, he said nothing about any judgments that would take place, but rather of power and dominion and the transfer of authority. "Daniel in his seventh chapter speaks of the Ancient of Days," he said. "He means the oldest man, our Father Adam, Michael; he will call his children together and hold a council with them to prepare them for the coming of the Son of Man.

"He (Adam) is the father of the human family, and presides over the spirits of all men, and all that have had the keys must stand before him in this grand council . . . The Son of Man stands before him, and there is given him glory and dominion. Adam delivers up his stewardship to Christ, that which was delivered to him as holding the keys of the universe, but retains his standing as head of the human family."[27]

Again, there is no mention of any opening of the books or the conducting of judgment. The main reason for holding the meeting at Adam-ondi-Ahman will be to conduct a council in which to prepare "for the coming of the Son of Man." Certain things need to be done ahead of time, however, including people making reports to Adam and delivering up stewardships or assignments of responsibility. Adam in turn will then deliver his own stewardship to Christ. It will be a grand and noble operation according to the order and system of the priesthood that will officially place the keys of administration and leadership in the hands of one individual. Everything will be in preparation for the time of the Second Coming.

Indeed the things which Daniel saw in his dream were extraordinary and of monumental importance, and they left him bewildered and with many questions. "I Daniel was grieved in my spirit in the midst of my body, and the visions of my head troubled me . . . As for me Daniel," he confessed, "my cogitations much troubled me, and my countenance changed in me: but I kept the matter in my heart."[28]

Surely the event in Adam-ondi-Ahman will be a momentous occasion, and it is an occurrence in the future to look forward to. But an important question that is always present is the number of people that will be there. How many people will be invited and eligible to attend? Because of what is depicted in the first part of Daniel's dream, some are of the opinion that a hundred million people or more will be in attendance. Yet anyone who has been in the Valley of Adam-ondi-Ahman and walked through it will undoubtedly agree that this is no area that would accommodate that many people, a number comparable to one-third of the United States' population. Even if areas several miles away might be considered as part of a so-called land of Adam-ondi-Ahman, the number of one hundred million is still too overwhelming.

The likelihood, and something more logical, is that the predicted gathering and meeting in this particular valley will be a secret and unobserved event. A relatively small number of people will be there, as far as a general population is concerned, and yet at the same time it will be regarded as a huge multitude that is in attendance, all by appointment and special invitation. It definitely will be what might be termed a priesthood meeting or solemn assembly. All those in past dispensations of the gospel, from the time of Adam to the present, who have possessed the highest and most important keys pertaining to the priesthood, will be there to make reports and deliver up stewardships. Without question it will be a very private affair, albeit a very large one, and it will come and go secretly and "as a thief in the night" as prophesied in Doctrine and Covenants 106:4.

To those in attendance, it will be a signal that the Lord's second advent is imminent, that everything is on schedule, and that important occurrences lie just ahead. In the final sequence of events, it will be only a short time before the beginning of the last countdown. It will also be one of the final signs that the seventh thousand years of the earth's temporal existence are well under way and that the earth will soon be plagued with a series of devastations and eventually be burned with fire!

One of the most interesting sections of the Bible contains the verses in the book of Revelation that tell about the opening of the seventh seal. John sees the events that will unfold right after the seal is opened. He tells of the one-half hour of silence that takes place, following which seven angels are given their trumpets. Another angel then appears and stands at the altar of the temple. The angel has "a golden censer; and there was given unto him much incense, that he should offer it with the prayers of all saints upon the golden altar which was before the throne. And the smoke of the incense, which came with the prayers of the saints, ascended up before God out of the angel's hand. And the angel took the censer, and filled it with fire of the altar, and cast it into the earth: and there were voices, and thunderings, and lightnings, and an earthquake."[29]

In wording that is very brief but filled with suspense and emotion, the scriptures tell of the time when the seven angels waiting at the temple are finally given permission to start sounding their trumpets. The strategic signal which will commence the final stages before the Second Coming and the final countdown of concluding events is about to occur. Indeed it is a deciding and historic moment. "And the seven angels which had the seven trumpets prepared themselves to sound."[29]

It is in the Doctrine and Covenants once again where a scriptural comment is made concerning the various events which follow, events that are also described in the book of Revelation and are a prelude to when the Lord comes in the clouds of glory. "And the sounding of the trumpets of the seven angels," the scripture says, "[is] the preparing and finishing of his work, in the beginning of the seventh thousand years—the preparing of the way before the time of his coming."[30]

As each angel sounds his trumpet, certain future events and conditions are briefly described, often in symbolic language. It is not until the fourth angel appears that a description is given that is more simply worded and refers to a more familiar topic, one similar to the phenomenon of sun, moon, and stars, yet also noticeably different. "And the fourth angel sounded," the scripture states, "and the third part of the sun was smitten, and the third part of the moon, and the third part of the stars; so as the third part of them was darkened, and the day shone not for a third part of it, and the night likewise."[31]

In regard to another angel, who was sixth in line to sound his trumpet, there is language that is again more easily understood, descriptions referring unmistakably to the time of Armageddon and the several years of battle which will take place in Palestine. It is in this account, in fact, that a giant earthquake occurs and two witnesses or prophets are killed in the city of Jerusalem. It is interesting to note that during another time when angels go forth with the seven last plagues, pouring their vials of wrath upon the earth, it is the fourth and sixth angels once again who are respectively associated with a type of sky phenomenon and also the famous battle.

Among the events and circumstances described by the seven angels with trumpets, as well as the angels carrying the small vessels or vials, there are events referring specifically to the unusual occurrences in the sky and the highly publicized battle in the area of Jerusalem and the Valley of Armageddon. Both of these are well-known subjects in scripture and have often been topics of speculation and controversy. It is not surprising that they are also two of the seven events of the final countdown which will occur in the future and precede the appearance and Second Coming of Jesus Christ!

Before a countdown ever begins, an unprecedented number of astronomical occurrences will take place as a prelude to the extraordinary sky phenomenon in the future. Some of these have already occurred, with others undoubtedly yet to come. One occurrence during modern times was reported by Joseph Smith.

On one occasion he had an unusual experience related to the idea of falling stars. The date was November 13, 1833. Being awakened in the nighttime by a neighbor, he went outside to see, as he later recorded in his journal, "the stars fall from heaven like a shower of hailstones."

"All heaven seemed enwrapped in splendid fireworks," he said, "as if every star in the broad expanse had been suddenly hurled from its course and sent lawless through the wilds of ether. Some at times appeared like bright shooting meteors, with long trains of light following in their course, and in numbers resembled large drops of rain in sunshine. These seemed to vanish when they fell behind the trees, or came near the ground. Some of the long trains of light following the meteoric stars, were visible for some seconds; these streaks would curl and twist up like serpents writhing. The appearance was beautiful, grand, and sublime beyond description; and it seemed as if the artillery and fireworks of eternity were set in motion."

Joseph Smith wrote in his journal following this unusual event. "Beautiful and terrific as was the scenery," he said. "It will not fully compare with the time when the sun shall become black like sackcloth of hair, the moon like blood, and the stars fall to the earth."[32]

Another account, briefly recorded by a historian on this same occasion states that "during the fall of 1833 occurred a natural phenomenon of a most wonderful character. This was on the night of the 13th of November. It is what is known as the 'meteoric shower' or the 'falling of the stars.' It was witnessed with amazement and astonishment throughout the entire limits of the United States."[33]

Once again, the idea expressed by Joseph Smith, and one implied by the scriptures themselves, is that far ahead in the last days, stars appearing to fall from the sky will be of a frequency and intensity that will set it apart from all previous occurrences. Apparently it will be a difficult event to comprehend. Yet in the meantime, there will have been other people, including those in ancient times, who, like Joseph Smith and many others, have witnessed unusual phenomena in the sky and interpreted them as significant signs in the heavens. One of these signs took place during the early part of the sixth century BC, and the other more recently in the time of Columbus.

On May 28, 585 BC, as recorded in history, a solar eclipse occurred during a battle between Media and Lydia in what is now central Turkey. The two nations had been disputing over territory for five years, and only a sudden eclipse of the sun caused them to finally stop and declare a truce. Interpreting the eclipse as a bad sign or omen, the invading Median army turned around and returned home.

Much later, in the beginning of the sixteenth century, another noteworthy eclipse took place, this time of the moon. It happened after Columbus had arrived in the New World and was marooned for many weeks on the island of Jamaica. The year was 1504.

The story is told how the natives on the island were unfriendly and did not want to give Columbus any food. He warned them, however, and said that if they refused, he would turn off the light in the sky at night. The explorer knew by his almanac that there was to be a lunar eclipse on February 29, 1504, and he predicted such an occurrence on that date to the natives. Of course they did not know what was going on, and when the eclipse arrived on schedule, it is said that they were terrified and begged Columbus to give them back the light, in return for which they would give him all the food that he needed.

Today eclipses of the sun and moon are of no great consequence, but in former times it was much different. Even at present, such unexplained phenomena as UFOs still cause people to wonder and speculate.

Again, all of these occurrences are merely a prelude to much greater events still to come. The conditions and circumstances created by modern technology are those which have been prophesied in both ancient and modern scripture. "And I will shew wonders in the heavens and in the earth," said the prophet Joel, "blood, and fire, and pillars of smoke."[34]

"And there shall be signs in the sun, and in the moon, and in the stars," as recorded in the gospel of Luke.[35] It will certainly be an impressive panorama of events, a dramaric introduction, and a grand preliminary to a final countdown. In a sensational display of phenomena relating to the sky, events of tremendous importance are heralded by a host of signs and wonders.

Almost supernatural and unbelievable at times, the signs emerge dramatically upon the stage of history in the final act of a drama which started at a place on the North American continent six thousand years ago. After six millennia, the last countdown, beginning at the historic and symbolic number seven, now commences with the remarkable return of the lost tribes of Israel, meaning their modern-day descendants, their exact identity having been unknown for more than twenty-six centuries!

The Final Countdown

7. Following centuries of isolation in a remote area, the lost tribes return in a miraculous manner.

6. The Battle of Armageddon takes place in the area of Jerusalem and the Valley of Esdraelon or Jezreel.

5. A gigantic earthquake, a type heretofore unknown, occurs along with other quakes, breaking down the mountains and shaking the nations.

4. In a wide sweep of transformation, the lands of Jerusalem and Zion are "turned back into their own place," and the earth's surface is changed.

3. The phenomenon of sun, moon, and stars is seen in the sky, and eventually also the sign of the Son of man.

2. The waters of the great deep, involving the seas and oceans, are "driven back into the north countries."

1. The "curtain of heaven" is unfolded, and the face of the Lord is revealed.

At this point, the Second Coming and what has been called the morning of the first resurrection will take place! Then sometime during this general time period, a worldwide burning of the earth will occur, followed by the commencement of the Millennium. Surely the confluence of so many important events in what has been referred to as the end of the world is almost beyond comprehension, but it will all happen eventually, and everything that has been predicted will in its own due time take place!

But first there is the countdown, the seven events of which are tentative and theoretical in their sequence but, in any case, begin with the return of the ten lost tribes of Israel. Somewhere in the northern part of the globe, in an area that has been designated in scripture as the north countries, this exotic group of people representing a lost civilization is scheduled to appear unexpectedly. In an unconventional manner, as described in religious prophecy, they will come from one location to another through some type of aperture or opening, first through a barrier of rock and then through one of ice, after which they will traverse a large expanse of water by way of some type of highway. Their destination reportedly will be a city in western Missouri called Zion.

Much like the children of Israel during the time of Moses who came out of Egypt and passed through the opening created for them in the Red Sea, these modern descendants of Israel will then begin a trek of several hundred miles that will eventually lead them to a promised land. In a way characteristic of pioneering groups in other time periods, they will travel through unknown territory, leaving everything they have known behind them and accepting whatever might be in store for the future. Their journey will be eventful and undoubtedly much different from the one they took when they came from their original location, a region where they were isolated and undetected for centuries.

In some ways, they will be a familiar and recognizable people, and although originating in a very different culture and environment, they will be Israelites nevertheless, possessing a rich biblical heritage as members of an institution that had its formal beginning on earth in the time of Abraham, Isaac, and Jacob, the latter also being known as Israel. It was Israel who had twelve sons, according to the book of Genesis, each of whom became the head of a tribe and eventually, with their father and descendants, traveled into Egypt during a time of famine. Certainly the origin of what has been called the House of Israel is well documented in the Bible, and a familiarity with it is important in regard to what it was that happened to the lost tribes.

The history of this illustrious society of people is one of the most notable in the annals of scripture. However, it was not until hundreds of years had passed, after they had become an independent nation and relocated to the promised land in Palestine, that they were recognized as a significant group. It was during the administration of the first three kings—Saul, David, and Solomon—that they became successful and were regarded as an important identity in the Middle East.

But when Solomon died, the kingdom he and his predecessors had built fell apart. In approximately 930 BC, it was divided into two groups. One was called the kingdom of Judah and was located in the south and ruled by Solomon's son Rehoboam. The other was the kingdom of Israel and was located in the north and led by a man named Jeroboam. Basically, one and one-half tribes stayed with Rehoboam while ten and one-half plus the priestly tribe of Levi rebelled and went with Jeroboam. A short time later, Levi changed back to the original group, leaving ten and one-half tribes in the north. These tribes became known in history as the ten tribes.

The two kingdoms remained as separate groups after the division, Israel being guided by a series of nineteen kings and Judah by twenty. During this time, they were often in conflict with one another, yet eventually both were conquered by people from the north. In the year 721 BC, armies from Assyria completed a conquest they had started several years earlier, and it was then that the northern kingdom became the first of the two Israelite nations to come to an end. A large part of the population was deported to various locations in the Assyrian Empire, and foreign colonists were brought in to take their place.

For the next century, the deported tribes spent their captivity in places the Bible describes as Hara, Halah, Habor by the river of Gozan, and the cities of the Medes. The biblical terminology in relation to Habor is more accurately expressed as "a town, city, or province named Gozan or Guzana situated on the river Khabur."[36] The first three of these areas were in the upper reaches of the Tigris and Euphrates Rivers in Mesopotamia, and the other further east beyond Assyria in Media.

The tribes generally appear to have been successful during the time they spent as prisoners, their situation under Assyrian rule often proving to be much better than that of people who had remained in Transjordan and Palestine. But in approximately 600 BC, an undetermined number in Assyria and Media banded together with the idea of leaving their places of captivity and migrating into the north country. Their alleged purpose was to find an area that was uninhabited, one where they could have privacy and be more devout in practicing their religion, something they had not always done before.

Evidently the main reason they were vulnerable to Assyrian invasions and conquest in the first place, as suggested in the Bible, and why so many were deported to foreign lands, was because of their long history of disobedience in regard to religion. Consequently, as they planned to go northward, identifying what it was they wanted to do, this was what was uppermost in their minds. The only explanation of what happened at that time is in the noncanonical record known as the Apocrypha.

"But they formed this plan for themselves," the record states, "that they would leave the multitude of the nations and go to a more distant region where mankind had never lived, that there at least they might keep their statutes which they had not kept in their own land."[37]

It is unfortunate that there is such a small amount of information concerning one of the important turning points in history, and that what we do know is contained in a source so questionable in its validity as the Apocrypha. As to its authenticity and reliability, however, a tentative endorsement is found in the Doctrine and Covenants where it says that "there are many things contained therein that are true, and it is mostly translated correctly." But the record also cautions that "there are many things contained therein that are not true, which are interpolations by the hands of men."[38]

As to the statement pertaining to the tribes in Assyria who are said to have migrated further north, the account can only be taken as it is written, with the idea that it is one of the things that is accurate and true. In any case, it is the only scriptural material telling about the ten tribes and their departure to the north country. Moreover, it is the one that also briefly describes their journey northward.

"And they went in by the narrow passages of the Euphrates River," the record says. "For at that time the Most High performed signs for them and stopped the channels of the river until they had passed over. Through that region there was a long way to go, a journey of a year and a half; and that country is called Arzareth."[39]

The whereabouts and present status of the ten tribes who went into the north countries continue to be a mystery, and it has often come to be a topic of conversation as to where they might be. It is also a common opinion that the topic is one which should generally be left alone since it is surrounded by so much conjecture and speculation. There are more important things to do, in other words, than talking in circles about the location of the ten lost tribes of Israel.

And yet there is something about this particular subject that makes it hard to set aside. The lack of knowledge and information can easily turn into bothersome questions, and the only way to get rid of them, if that is possible, is to try to find the answers, or at least form an enlightened opinion supported by the facts which are available and the best of circumstantial evidence. There is also the realization that this is much more than just a topic of conversation. It is part of the phenomenon known as the scattering and gathering of Israel. It is the idea that Israelites down through history have been moved to new lands or dispersed among the nations, at the same time being given the promise that they will be gathered again and be reunited. According to religious prophecy, the lost tribes are one of those groups and will someday be restored to their original lands of inheritance.

In the meantime, they remain hidden in some remote and undisclosed area. The only clue as to their location is that they last traveled through a region called Arzareth. This was far removed from their original starting point in Mesopotamia and might have been one of the places the prophet Jeremiah referred to in the Bible when he referred to the north country. But wherever the tribes are at present, there is definitely a scriptural implication that at least some of them are on the alert, giving heed to what their leaders are telling them and waiting for the time when a signal is given saying that the date has finally arrived for them to move to a new location!

The most common opinion as to where the lost tribes might be located is that they are currently dispersed and scattered throughout the world, disseminated among the nations. Like corn sifted in a sieve, as viewed by the Old Testament prophet Amos, they are intermingled among the peoples of the world and distributed worldwide. "For, lo, I will command," he said, speaking for the Lord, "and I will sift the house of Israel among all nations, like as corn is sifted in a sieve, yet shall not the least grain fall upon the earth."[40]

According to one survey, the main theory relating to the location of the lost tribes is the Dispersion Theory. Of more than two hundred people who were polled, fifty-three percent said they thought the tribes were presently dispersed among the nations of the world. Another view, the Unknown Planet Theory, was that they occupy a position much like the City of Enoch in the Bible, in that they have been transported to another planet or sphere. Twenty-nine percent favored this idea.

Eleven percent of the people believed in a North Pole Theory, an opinion placing the tribes in some kind of hidden area in the polar regions. Another four percent accepted the possibility of a hollow earth, and two percent gave a personal theory of their own.[41]

Of course whether one or the other of these theories is closer to the truth is undoubtedly a subject for debate, and yet in some ways it is also relatively unimportant. The main facts involved are that the tribes actually do exist somewhere and that someday they will be gathered and will return. Everything else is mostly opinion and speculation. Concerning a dispersion among the nations, however, which seems to be the most prevalent view, the evidence generally suggests that this particular theory, although a popular one, is very possibly incorrect, at least in regard to the portion of tribes that was taken captive into Assyria.

It was Assyrian policy during this time period not to deport the entire population of a certain region but only about one-half or less. Then by bringing in colonists from other areas to take their place, the new rulers weakened the existing social structure and were able to maintain stronger control. Those who were not deported were eventually dispersed among the nations. But the tribes that were taken captive, or at least the group that migrated farther into the north countries, allegedly escaped dispersion and consequently remained separate from the others. This is the group that eventually disappeared from the regular run of society and became known as the lost tribes of Israel.

Wherever the tribes are at present, they appear to be a separate and distinct group, most likely a nation or group of nations, and at least some of them are a religious people. From time to time there have been prophets among them, and these men will someday be given the signal when it is finally time for the tribes to return. It is the nature of that return, however, that will be unusual and miraculous, enough so that to hear a description of it in advance might seem unbelievable. At the same time, such a report could also be a verification of its own validity, as well as a clue as to where the tribes are located.

There appears to be no way that a completely rational explanation can be given to identify the whereabouts of the lost tribes of Israel. From the outset, allowances have to be made, especially in this particular situation. The idea must be accepted ahead of time that because of the nature of the subject, miraculous circumstances will undoubtedly be involved.

The present location of the tribes, along with their predicted return, is in the same category as the miracles of the New Testament, such as Jesus walking on water, mysteriously appearing and disappearing among people, and rising off the ground into mid air. It is the same kind of phenomena as Moses parting the waters of the Red Sea and Joshua causing the sun and moon to stand still. Certainly all of these are remarkable occurrences and are part of the supernatural aspect of scripture which is so characteristic of the Bible.

But in connection with the lost tribes, how they disappeared and where they are, as well as how they will return, the answers will probably never be known until there is new information or divine revelation. Since it is said that the people involved were guided by God himself from the beginning, only he can say for certain what it was that happened to them. In the meantime, there will always be a question, along with the inevitable plethora of theory and speculation.

And yet history again can provide a possible answer, or at least a compromise, and certain scriptural information hints strongly at a conclusion. The deportation policies of the Assyrian Empire, for example, give a clue as to where at least one portion of the tribes is located. The Doctrine and Covenants gives another possibility concerning the location of a second portion.

Because the Assyrians deported only one-half or less of a conquered city or region, it follows that the one-half which remained in the Palestine area would eventually mix with incoming colonists and ultimately intermingle with people in other countries. This would identify the location of one portion of the ten tribes, those who were not taken into captivity but stayed in their original homeland, and at the same time partially verify the claim by many that the tribes are currently dispersed throughout the nations.

But the question of what happened to the group of captives in Assyria, especially those who banded together and disappeared into the north country, presents a more difficult problem, one that appears to have no reliable solution without the intervention of a significant source of outside information. And in this case, it is the Doctrine and Covenants once again that presents a valuable clue. Only in this one source is there material indicating where the tribes might be located, in what manner they will return, and possibly how they disappeared from the land of Arzareth in the first place. In just a few verses of scripture, answers are given to a significant number of questions.

In relation to the tribes and how they will return someday, the record gives valuable information. "And they who are in the north countries shall come in remembrance before the Lord," it says, "and their prophets shall hear his voice, and shall no longer stay themselves; and they shall smite the rocks, and the ice shall flow down at their presence. And an highway shall be cast up in the midst of the great deep."[42]

Sometime in the future, a divine command will be given for the tribes to return. Prophets among them will "no longer stay themselves" or continue waiting for a signal to rejoin normal society, but will eventually make their way with their particular congregations to a place of exit. At this point, wherever it turns out to be, miraculous events will occur, much like the time when the Lord performed signs on the bank of the Euphrates River and Moses parted the waters of the Red Sea.

The prophets leading the people, according to the scripture, will "smite the rocks" and create some type of breach or opening through which the returning tribes will pass. A clue as to their general geographic location is given by the reference to ice that "will flow down at their presence." It is then that a highway or some kind of elevated passageway will be raised up out of the sea in front of them in order for a potentially large number of people to proceed further toward a destination.

In a scene that is again reminiscent of the children of Israel crossing the Red Sea, a throng of modern Israelites will traverse a large body of water, coming out of the north countries and heading toward the south. Their objective will be a new city called Zion, or the New Jerusalem, on the North American continent. There they will be welcomed by another group of Israelites, those specifically who are descendants of the tribe of Ephraim.

Whereas the ten tribes have a general ancestry from all of the tribes except Judah and possibly Levi, those awaiting them in Zion will be by direct lineage or adoption mainly from one particular group and will be called the children of Ephraim. They are the ones who will not only welcome the incoming tribes but will bestow upon them some type of glory, a spiritual gift or endowment. At the same time, those returning will bring with them their own gifts and treasures.

"And they shall bring forth their rich treasures unto the children of Ephraim, my servants," states the scripture, quoting the Lord, "and the boundaries of the everlasting hills shall tremble at their presence. And there shall they fall down and be crowned with glory, even in Zion, by the hands of the servants of the Lord, even the children of Ephraim.

"And they shall be filled with songs of everlasting joy. Behold, this is the blessing of the everlasting God upon the tribes of Israel, and the richer blessing upon the head of Ephraim and his fellows."[42]

Surely these will be important events, involving unusual conditions and circumstances. It is also significant that a description of the tribes returning in the future gives a clue as to how they disappeared from the land of Arzareth in the past. The conditions of their disappearance, in other words, might well have been similar to those predicted for their return, including the features of rock, ice, and water at the place of exit, along with an unusual highway or passageway.

But one thing appears certain, according to the account in the Apocrypha, and that is that as the tribes originally began the journey from Assyria to Arzareth, there was a supernatural occurrence as they prepared to cross the Euphrates River. "For at that time the Most High performed signs for them and stopped the channels of the river until they had passed over."[43] At the very beginning there were extraordinary circumstances, as well as at the end when they reached a preliminary destination and embarkation point. The implication is that it was here that they experienced a supernatural phenomenon that enabled them to enter a new area within the confines of the earth, conditions being comparable once again to those their descendants would encounter when exiting many centuries in the future.

To fully comprehend what has happened, or will happen, on all of these occasions requires not only an act of intellect but also one of faith. Certainly it is not always easy to visualize the occurrence of such things, and it is understandable when a person chooses to interpret certain situations figuratively or symbolically rather than literally. Whereas in some scripture this proves to be the correct way, in those pertaining to the lost tribes it is often not the correct solution. A good way to achieve something which is commonplace and generic is to simplify it by reducing it down to a level that is less complicated and abstract, but in doing it is possible that the true significance and meaning of something will be lost.

It has been said that people tend to explain away in literal simplicity what they do not wish to understand. This is particularly true in regard to the miraculous occurrences pertaining to the ten tribes. This tendency also relates to the circumstances of their present location, whether they are in isolation and hidden away in a remote and obscure place or are dispersed and disseminated among the nations.

A noted scientist and theologian once commented on these things, first on the idea of miraculous occurrences and then specifically on the return of the lost tribes. In response to those who believe that the tribes have been dispersed and are presently being gathered in different countries of the world, and "that we are not to look for the return of any body of people now unknown as to their whereabouts," his comments included the following: "True, the gathering is now in progress," he said. "This is a gathering dispensation. But the prophecy stands that the tribes shall be brought forth from their hiding place, bringing their scriptures with them."[44]

At the time it seemed like an unusual statement to make, but very clear nevertheless in its meaning. Obviously the reference to a "hiding place" might have sounded strange and unfamiliar to some, but still these were the words he used. And in actuality, a place of hiding and seclusion, shrouded by uncertainty and mystery, is possibly the correct terminology, aptly stated and expressing the current existence of a remarkable and extraordinary group of people.

Somewhere in the confines of the earth, at a place traditionally associated with the land of the north, the lost tribes of Israel do exist as a nation. They are not intermingled among the different countries of the world, as some might suppose, but are living as a separate group of people at an undisclosed location. Unlike in times past, very little is said about them anymore, and on occasion when the subject of their return is mentioned, it is almost regarded as fiction. Yet in the future, when the rumor comes that crumbling rock and flowing ice have opened up a passageway in the north countries and a mysterious highway has appeared, then will people know that the ten tribes are real and are finally on their way!

As the time draws near to when the Second Coming takes place, the return of the lost tribes will be an impressive and significant event, terminating a long period of absence and isolation. But the occurrence of what has come to be known as the Battle of Armageddon, a future event dreaded and anticipated for centuries, is equally impressive. Undoubtedly it is something that will be extraordinary and unparalleled, a conflict synonymous with the idea of climax and the end of the world.

At a time when the world in its recorded history is approaching the Millennium, this battle alone will be unrivaled in its intensity and will represent the eventual end of armed hostility and warfare. Any fighting occurring up until the time of the earth's burning will be of no consequence in comparison. Traditionally the battle is regarded as a type of war that has never happened before and without question has become a symbol of the ultimate conflict. The very sound and pronunciation of its name conjure up ominous and threatening images.

The fact that it occurs just prior to the end of the world gives it a priority and notoriety that set it apart as a dramatic and spectacular event. And although the word *Armageddon* itself appears only once in all of scripture, namely in the book of Revelation, it is a powerful name, denoting things not only relating to war and conflict but also to those that are religious and apocalyptic. The Battle of Armageddon, in fact, will basically be a religious war, testing one ideology and way of life against another and involving people from many different cultures and backgrounds.

Despite the fact that the Bible does not specifically refer to any one group of people engaging in conflict with one another, rather the idea that it is God himself in opposition with the forces of evil, the overall impact of scripture is still that someday there will be a concluding battle. People from all of the major nations will be involved on that occasion, participating in a conflict that will commence in or near the Valley of Megiddo in Palestine. As to what will happen and how it will begin, the best source of information is found in scripture.

In dramatic wording similar to that in the book of Revelation which talks about the seven angels preparing to sound their trumpets, the same book speaks mysteriously of such things as "the spirits of devils, working miracles, which go forth unto the kings of the earth and of the whole world, to gather them to the battle of that great day of God Almighty." And whereas this again might be referring to God's contest with evil forces, it also can be regarded as the genesis of a famous battle.

"And he gathered them together," the scripture says, "into a place called in the Hebrew tongue Armageddon."[45]

The Valley of Megiddo is situated near the city of the same name and has sometimes been referred to as the Valley of Jezreel and the Plain of Esdraelon, as well as the Valley of Armageddon. It is a narrow passageway in northern Palestine coming in from the Plain of Sharon on the Mediterranean coast. The passage has been used by armies and caravans for centuries and was a convenient and expedient shortcut across the Jezreel Valley to the area of the Jordan River. Located on the caravan route from Egypt to Damascus in Syria, it has also been the battleground of nations for many hundreds of years and in the future will be the general area where the Battle of Armageddon will originate. In the annals of history it is a foreboding place, in striking contrast with its present landscape of peaceful surroundings and fertile crops and fields.

Considering its history, it is certainly not surprising that this same geographical area should end up the selected locale for a final battleground of nations. Men and equipment will someday converge on this area from all over the world, especially from locations in the north countries, and massive military operations will extend from the Jezreel Valley and Plain of Esdraelon to the city of Jerusalem fifty miles to the south. Although the actual combat will undoubtedly be more extended and widespread, the immediate focus of the war will be in northern and central Palestine.

In the book of Ezekiel, one of the most important sources of information on this topic, there is a mysterious reference to Gog, "the chief prince of Meshech and Tubal,"[46] who in the last days will lead a giant army out of the north country in a widespread attack on Palestine. At that time many other groups will join him, and together they will move across the land like a storm. The biblical record states that in those days it will be many nations of the world combined against the Jewish people who are living upon the mountains of Israel.

Scholars and historians have given their opinions on what will happen, but in no place is there a more interesting and impressive account than that which is recorded in scripture. It is an event prophesied not only in the book of Ezekiel but in other sources as well, including the books of Joel, Zechariah, and Revelation. Consequently the battle action is always viewed from an ancient standpoint, the writers being unfamiliar with modern invention and technology, which without question will be an important part of the conflict.

In comparison with other wars, the Battle of Armageddon in many ways will be the worst that the world has ever known. Although the weaponry and means of warfare might not always be highly sophisticated, the intensity of fighting will be unparalleled. In the words of the prophet Joel, "there hath not been ever the like, neither shall be any more after it, even to the years of many generations."[47]

At the time of this great battle, the forces of Gog will come down from the north out of the land called Magog, which traditionally is the same as ancient Scythia near the upper parts of the Black and Caspian Seas. In a modern world known for its high technology and scientific achievement, many of the invaders will appear as in days of old, "all of them riding upon horses, a great company, and a mighty army."[48]

This will not be any ordinary invasion. The intent of the aggressor will be to conquer Israel and destroy it! After building up in the Middle East for centuries, the bitterness and hatred toward the Jewish people will suddenly break loose in a huge onslaught of mounted warriors. From many nations in different parts of the world, including Iran (ancient Persia), Libya, and Ethiopia, they will gather around Gog their leader, "all of them clothed with all sorts of armour, even a great company with bucklers and shields, all of them handling swords."[49] And in one gigantic thrust, the invading armies will cover the land like a cloud.

According to Joel's prophecy, it will be a time of great trouble, "a day of darkness and of gloominess, a day of clouds and of thick darkness . . . A fire devoureth before them," the prophet says, "and behind them a flame burneth: the land is as the garden of Eden before them, and behind them a desolate wilderness; yea, and nothing shall escape them."[50]

But all of this will be to no avail, as far as Gog and his forces are concerned. Following two major earthquakes in and around Jerusalem, one claiming the lives of seven thousand people and the other "such as was not since men were upon the earth, so mighty an earthquake, and so great,"[51] the Lord himself will intervene, and with a rain of hailstones, fire, and brimstone, he will bring the devastating invasion to an end. A countless number of men and animals will fall on that fateful day, and their bodies will cover the open fields.

Especially in Jerusalem, there will be a dramatic end to the battle. After being overrun by enemy forces, and when everything seems to be lost, the Jewish people will be delivered in a spectacular and supernatural manner as the Lord Jesus Christ appears and stands upon the Mount of Olives across from the city.

At that moment, according to the book of Zechariah, the mount will cleave in the center toward the east and toward the west, one half shifting to the north and the other to the south, providing a miraculous pathway of escape. The people in the city will then flee to "the valley of the mountains,"[52] and much like the parting of the Red Sea when Moses led the Hebrews out of Egypt, a cataclysmic separation of land will now save a similar group, the embattled inhabitants of Jerusalem and the modern-day descendants of ancient Israel.

This one occurrence, apart from everything else, stands out above all others during the Battle of Armageddon. It is the surprising climax which will bring all fighting and aggression to an end. It is also the event, among several others, that will precede the Second Coming and be a prelude to the long-awaited Millennium!

As to the battle account itself, there is admittedly much of the action which is symbolic and representative of things as they existed anciently, but at the same time there is much also that is actual and literal, and it would be a mistake not to recognize these areas, whichever they might be. Moreover, it is noteworthy that the Mount of Olives incident, which is definitely a literal occurrence, is not the final appearance of the Lord that commences the Millennium but merely a preliminary leading to that event. There will be an undetermined number of years immediately following the battle, for example, when many important events will take place, one of them being an occurrence that constitutes a grim and solemn epilogue to all that has happened. After the conflict has ended and all fighting has come to an end, and before the Jewish people start clearing away the refuse and burying the dead, a strange and unusual type of feast, very graphically described in the Bible, will be held in Palestine.

The Lord will invite every feathered fowl and every beast of the field to assemble themselves together upon the battlegrounds for a great sacrifice that he has prepared for them. It will be an invitation to attend a banquet, as it were, and to eat at the royal table. In fact, this future event is referred to in scripture not only as the summons to a sacrifice, but also as an invitation to attend the Lord's supper.

To all the fowls and beasts he will say, "Come and gather yourselves together unto the supper of the great God."[53] He will go on to say, "Assemble yourselves, and come; gather yourselves on every side to my sacrifice that I do sacrifice for you, even a great sacrifice upon the mountains of Israel, that ye may eat flesh, and drink blood.

"Ye shall eat the flesh of the mighty, and drink the blood of the princes of the earth . . . And ye shall eat fat till ye be full, and drink blood till ye be drunken, of my sacrifice which I have sacrificed for you. Thus ye shall be filled at my table with horses and chariots, with mighty men, and with all men of war, saith the Lord God."[54]

It is only after all of this has been accomplished that the people of Palestine will then start cleansing the land, clearing away the weapons and removing the dead. It will take seven months to bury Gog and his armies in a valley by the sea, and the weapons recovered from the battlegrounds will provide fuel to burn for seven years.

"And they that dwell in the cities of Israel shall go forth, and shall set on fire and burn the weapons, both the shields and the bucklers, the bows and the arrows, and the handstaves, and the spears, and they shall burn them with fire seven years: So that they shall take no wood out of the field, neither cut down any out of the forests; for they shall burn the weapons with fire."[55]

As to the burial of the dead, the Bible states that "all the people of the land shall bury them." For a time it will be a community enterprise, and the vast cemetery for an innumerable number of soldiers will be in a valley at the eastern end of the Mediterranean Sea. "And there shall they bury Gog and all his multitude: and they shall call it The Valley of Hamon gog."[55] There will also be a city there called Hamonah.

Such will be the aftermath of a legendary but historical battle. The inevitable events related to this war are part of a continuing countdown leading to a consummation of world history and human affairs. Certainly these will be extraordinary occurrences showing that the latter days are rapidly drawing to a close and the Second Coming and Millennium are indeed imminent. While the historic Battle of Armageddon will prophetically be the most deadly of all conflicts, it is the dramatic event on the Mount of Olives when the Lord makes his sudden appearance that continues to be the symbol and remembrance of the war itself and of all the events which will have taken place! Surely it will be foremost among the final signs of the times, along with those already on the horizon, future occurrences that will transform the earth and dramatically change the complexion of the sky!

The cataclysm that causes the Mount of Olives to split and separate will be tremendous, "and the earth shall tremble, and reel to and fro, and the heavens also shall quake."[56] This particular quaking of the earth, however, is not the one referred to in the book of Revelation that will be unprecedented and unparalleled, one "such as was not since men were upon the earth." But it will be a phenomenal occurrence, nonetheless, which, along with similar incidents taking place during this same time period, will result in a long series of earthquakes and geologic upheavals. Indeed, especially as far as the Lord is concerned, it will be a time of testimony and retribution.

In reference to people whom he commissions as ministers, including prophets, evangelists, clergymen, and missionaries, the message and testimony involved will not only be one of admonition and instruction, but also one of warning. In consequence of wrong doing, in other words, there will be retribution, some of it caused by forces of nature.

"And after your testimony," the scripture says, addressing the religious emissaries, "cometh wrath and indignation upon the people. For after your testimony cometh the testimony of earthquakes, that shall cause groanings in the midst of her, and men shall fall upon the ground and shall not be able to stand. And also cometh the testimony of the voice of thunderings, and the voice of lightnings, and the voice of tempests, and the voice of the waves of the sea heaving themselves beyond their bounds. And all things shall be in commotion."[57]

The scriptures do not mention earthquakes too often, but three that are well known and of special interest are found in Revelation 6:12, 11:13, and 16:18. The first of these is listed among the four main events pertaining to the opening of the sixth seal; the last two refer to the Battle of Armageddon. It is these earthquakes in particular that are significant and in close proximity to the time of the Second Coming.

The quake assigned to the sixth seal, however, is an event that once again very possibly belongs to the seventh and is allegedly synonymous with the gigantic earthquake that will be unparalleled and unprecedented. Since at least two of the sixth seal events appear to be out of order chronologically (unquestionably relating to a later time period immediately preceding Christ's second advent), it follows that what is referred to as a great earthquake should possibly be listed with these two events as well.

Two major earthquakes, therefore, will likely occur toward the end of the Battle of Armageddon, and although they are sometimes viewed as a single event, their particular circumstances suggest otherwise. At a crucial point during the battle, for example, after Jerusalem has been under siege for several years, the bodies of two slain prophets which have been lying unburied in the city for three and a half days suddenly come to life again and ascend into heaven. It is then that there is "a great earthquake, and the tenth part of the city"[58] falls, a temblor causing the death of seven thousand people. It is not the end of the war at this point but nevertheless a scene of tragedy and desolation, characterized by the death of the two prophets. This is the earthquake mentioned in Revelation 11:13 and again appears to be separate from the one referred to in the text that follows it.

Apparently only a short time after this first quake, the city of Jerusalem and its environs will be hit by a second one, much more severe in intensity. This is the one described in Revelation 16:18 where an angel carrying the seventh and final vial of plagues pours its contents into the air. "And there were voices, and thunders, and lightnings," the scripture says, "and there was a great earthquake, such as was not since men were upon the earth, so mighty an earthquake, and so great." Again, this is also the quake alleged to be the one in the sixth seal. "And the great city was divided into three parts, and the cities of the nations fell."[59]

At the time of these two earthquakes, just prior to the conclusion of the Battle of Armageddon, it will be as if God himself were preparing the people for the end, serving notice and delivering the testimony of not just one natural disaster but two, and undoubtedly causing many more fatalities than just seven thousand people, especially among Gog and his forces in the area of the city of Jerusalem. And yet the battle will still continue for a time until the famous city and capital finally fall to the aggressor.

"For I will gather all nations against Jerusalem to battle," declares Zechariah the prophet, speaking on behalf of the Lord, "and the city shall be taken, and the houses rifled, and the women ravished; and half of the city shall go forth into captivity, and the residue of the people shall not be cut off from the city."[60]

It will be these two earthquakes, occurring in relatively close succession with one another, that will be a spectacular prelude to the closing stages of the Battle of Armageddon. These two events appear to be those immediately preceding the dramatic appearance of Jesus Christ on the Mount of Olives, and yet not before the city of Jerusalem is pillaged and desecrated and, in fulfillment of prophecy, "trodden down of the Gentiles."[61]

In connection with these events, the scripture stating that the second earthquake will be "such as was not since men were upon the earth" is extremely interesting since it will be a sequel to so many devastating quakes that have taken place in the past. The deadliest known earthquake on record, for example, occurred in the year 1556 in the Shaanxi province in China and reportedly killed 830,000 people. More recently was the giant temblor in Chili in 1960, registering 9.5 on the Moment magnitude scale, a type of measurement alleged to be newer and even more accurate than the Richter. This particular earthquake is said to be the largest ever recorded on earth and generated tsunamis all across the Pacific Ocean.

Finally, to say that there will be another earthquake in years to come much more powerful than any that have occurred so far gives only a small idea of the incredible shaking that is in store for the earth. Such an occurrence is definitely prophesied, however, and the gigantic quake described in the book of Revelation will reportedly be one without precedent.

Yet again it will be the spectacular event on the Mount of Olives when Christ makes his sudden appearance ending the Battle of Armageddon that will be the most extraordinary occurrence of all. Though the splitting of the mount at that time apparently will not be comparable in intensity to the giant earthquake preceding it, it will still be of much greater significance. Indeed, it is the specific event that some have interpreted as being part of the Lord's second advent itself, one where he appears in glory bringing all of the saints with him. And although the occurrence on the mount will be impressive, it is still not the Second Coming, many other important events still needing to take place in the future.

As far as earthquakes in general are concerned, along with the accompanying thunderings, lightnings, tempests, and the tsunamic waves of the sea, those in the land of Palestine in and around Jerusalem will undoubtedly only be a beginning. This is the time, in fact, when regions all over the world will continue to experience a phenomenal shaking of the land, one causing untold damage of property and loss of life, as well as what might be regarded as an actual reconstruction of the earth's surface and topography. It will definitely be a period of time when vast changes occur, and the world and its people will be challenged and affected in many different ways!

One of the most prominent prophecies in scripture, and at the same time the most alarming, says that someday there will be a great shaking of the earth, first in the land of Israel and eventually throughout the nations. It is one predicting that not only people and animal life will be affected but also that buildings and structures everywhere will be destroyed and "mountains shall be thrown down."[62] The countless quakes involved will theoretically be among the giant aftershocks of the massive earthquakes during the Battle of Armageddon.

"Surely in that day there shall be a great shaking in the land of Israel," according to the book of Ezekiel, "so that the fishes of the sea, and the fowls of the heaven, and the beasts of the field, and all creeping things that creep upon the earth, and all the men that are upon the face of the earth, shall shake at my presence, and the mountains shall be thrown down, and the steep places shall fall, and every wall shall fall to the ground."[62]

In a similar but more brief prophecy in the book of Haggai, the prophet states, "For thus saith the Lord of hosts; Yet once, it is a little while, and I will shake the heavens, and the earth, and the sea, and the dry land; and I will shake all nations."[63]

Unquestionably, there will come a time in the future when earthquakes take place not just as a testimony proclaiming

God's wrath and indignation, but as a way of altering and transforming the earth, eventually preparing it for a coming destiny. Predictions and prophecies pertaining to these events are found in scripture, referring first to a shaking of the earth and then to a later period of dissolution and burning, the former to occur before the Second Coming and the latter to happen after.

The shaking will be in connection with the earth in its temporal and telestial condition and the burning a preparation for one that is temporal and terrestrial or Millennial. Both are necessary in the earth's spiritual progression. The philosophy as recorded in scripture is that the earth itself is a living entity and is necessarily progressing through a series of steps leading to its own salvation and exaltation. As a consequence, the burning that occurs in the future will result in new heavens and a new earth, all in preparation for the Millennium.

But a gigantic shaking and rocking of the earth must first take place, and in the scriptures there are many references as to what will happen and what the consequences will be. Foremost among all of these are the prophecies of Isaiah.

"The windows from on high are open," he says, "and the foundations of the earth do shake. The earth is utterly broken down, the earth is clean dissolved, the earth is moved exceedingly. The earth shall reel to and fro like a drunkard, and shall be removed like a cottage."[64]

In another scripture Isaiah states the well-known description concerning the consequences. "Every valley shall be exalted," he writes, "and every mountain and hill shall be made low: and the crooked shall be made straight, and the rough places plain: and the glory of the Lord shall be revealed, and all flesh shall see it together: for the mouth of the Lord hath spoken it."[65]

Basically the same thing was recorded by Luke in the New Testament when he said, "Every valley shall be filled, and every mountain and hill shall be brought low; and the crooked shall be made straight, and the rough ways shall be made smooth. And all flesh shall see the salvation of God."[66]

In the Doctrine and Covenants, further details are given regarding what will happen in the latter days, especially how the earth will be shaken and appear as one who is drunken and reeling. "Wherefore, be not deceived, but continue in steadfastness," states the scripture, "looking forth for the heavens to be shaken, and the earth to tremble and to reel to and fro as a drunken man, and for the valleys to be exalted, and for the mountains to be made low, and for the rough places to become smooth—and all this when the angel shall sound his trumpet."[67]

"For not many days hence and the earth shall tremble and reel to and fro as a drunken man," according to still another scripture, "and the sun shall hide his face, and shall refuse to give light; and the moon shall be bathed in blood; and the stars shall become exceedingly angry and shall cast themselves down as a fig that falleth from off a fig-tree."[68]

But in section 133 of the Doctrine and Covenants, an extremely significant statement is made, not only one pertaining to mountains generally being thrown or broken down, but rather a solitary scriptural reference identifying one specific locality involved in a future transformation of the earth.

"And he shall utter his voice out of Zion," the scripture says, referring to the Lord, "and he shall speak from Jerusalem, and his voice shall be heard among all people; and it shall be a voice as the voice of many waters, and as the voice of a great thunder, which shall break down the mountains, and the valleys shall not be found . . . And the land of Jerusalem and the land of Zion shall be turned back into their own place, and the earth shall be like as it was in the days before it was divided."[69]

The reference to the lands of Jerusalem and Zion being "turned back into their own place" constitutes a remarkable statement, apparently relating at least in part to the phenomenal shaking and jolting of the earth that is predicted for the future. In order for the earth's geology and surface construction to return to the way it was before it was divided by all kinds of changes and transformations in the biblical days of Peleg, tremendous cataclysms need to occur, cataclysms without any kind of recorded precedent or parallel.

An example of this type of quaking or cataclysm would be an earthquake similar to the one scheduled to strike Palestine in the waning days of Armageddon, such an earthquake as has never happened before. And yet for the geological and geographical situation of the earth to return to the way it was originally, including the lands of Jerusalem and Zion, a tremendous rocking of the earth will need to take place, not just in one location but many. A theoretical sketch of what the earth's surface looks like beneath the Atlantic and Pacific Oceans, comprising deep chasms and extensive ruptures, gives only a limited idea of what kind of transformation will be necessary to restore the earth to the way it was in the beginning of human history.

When Adam and Eve were in the Garden of Eden, the geography and topography of the earth allegedly were much different from what they are today. In those days, after the waters had been gathered during the time of the Creation, there was a much smaller volume of seas and ocean. The movement of water, in fact, was generally to one specific location and resulted in a much smaller sea. As a consequence, the land surface stretched for thousands of miles in what actually amounted to one gigantic continent.

At that time, the lands of Jerusalem and Zion were still thousands of miles apart, being on opposite sides of the globe yet no longer separated by water. It would have been possible, in other words, to travel by foot or surface transportation back and forth between the two locations.

The assertion that the Garden of Eden was originally where the central part of the United States is now located could therefore very well be true, and had there been the right kinds of transportation anciently, great distances might have been covered. As to whether or not there were mountains to cross, or other such obstacles, and if so, what kind and how many—that is undetermined.

It is true that Isaiah said that every mountain and hill would be brought low, implying a continuously flat land surface, yet the complete meaning of such a statement and description is yet to be determined. The important idea is expressed in the Doctrine and Covenants where it says that the earth in the days ahead will be changed and "shall be like as it was in the days before it was divided."[69] What it is that will actually happen on that occasion is not completely known but continues to be an interesting part of the signs of the times. Those events and circumstances have been recorded by the prophets and are timely announced in the annals of scripture!

One way of viewing the earth, and what will take place on its surface in the future, is by way of a certain theory called the Law of Restoration, an idea stating that, among other things, the earth will someday be restored to its original condition. Common and familiar in some ways yet relatively unknown in others, it constitutes a significant concept and comprises several different aspects.

One part of the law, as it pertains to human beings, states that after people die, they will eventually be resurrected, at which time they will be restored to a proper frame and order. By way of this process, a perfected body will be restored to its spirit. In other words, the spirit will also be restored to the body, the two never again to be separated.

People at this time will be exempt from disease, death, and physical infirmities. Every part and function of the body, as well as conditions such as missing limbs, blindness, different kinds of deformity, and retardation, will be perfected. Everything will assume an ideal and natural state.

In another sense, involving a much more abstract and spiritual part of the law, each person in the world will also be rewarded according to the kind of life he or she has lived. There will be a restorative action in which someone who has led a good life will be restored to that which is good, while those who deliberately choose to do otherwise will be restored to the opposite. All of this is a vital part of the Law of Restoration, and if it were any other way, the demands of justice could not be fulfilled.

These physical and spiritual events are very important, each occurring in connection with a future resurrection, but there is also a third aspect of the law said to be now in progress. It is mentioned briefly in the New Testament when the apostle Peter refers to a type of restitution.

"And he shall send Jesus Christ, which before was preached unto you," he says, referring to the Lord's Second Coming, "whom the heaven must receive until the restitution of all things, which God has spoken by the mouth of all his holy prophets since the world began."[70]

This restitution, according to the interpretation of the Law of Restoration, means that many things pertaining to the gospel of Jesus Christ which have been discontinued or lost down through the ages are to be brought back sometime during the latter days. All of the religious principles and ordinances that were practiced during the times of Adam, Enoch, Noah, Abraham, and Moses, as well as during Christ's ministry, will at one time or another be restored to the earth in their fullness.

This belief, however, is not widely recognized and accepted. Most people, in fact, would probably classify it more as theory than anything else, regarding it as only one among many religious philosophies. The truth of it, as far as they are concerned, is yet to be established. In the meantime, despite any skepticism or doubt, it continues to be an interesting concept and in the field of religion stands as a detailed and explanatory doctrine.

A fourth part of the Law of Restoration pertains to what is referred to as the gathering of Israel, also allegedly taking place at the present time. It states that the descendants of the different tribes of the House of Israel, which have been scattered down through the centuries, are to be gathered together again in the last days and eventually restored to the lands of their inheritance. People of this particular lineage, including those who are adopted into it, will be an important motivating force as the world nears the time for entering the Millennium.

In conclusion, there is still one more part of this unusual law, one that is directly associated with the geologic and geographic transformation of the earth. It involves the idea that the earth is not only an astronomical and geological entity, but also a living organism with certain characteristics analogous to those of a human being.

From this perspective, it is said to have a spiritual nature along with one that is physical. Consequently, it can be viewed as much more than just a material object in the universe. As the spirit and body of an individual constitute the soul of man, for example, so might the combined spiritual and temporal parts of the planet be regarded as the soul of the earth.

This means that the earth, following its creation or birth, eventually entered a type of existence that, in some ways, is like that of a human being. It then began a progression through a series of stages that are spiritual as well as physical. From a religious standpoint, this included a baptism by water at the time of the great flood, and another baptism during a time period referred to as the end of the world, at which point there will be a baptism by fire. These two occurrences, in addition to being physical catastrophes and natural disasters, might also be considered types of religious ordinances.

It is in connection with a final baptism by fire that the earth will be cleansed and restored to a previous glory. And yet before that occurs, it will undergo transformation, with many hills and mountains being shaken and broken down. Again it will be the same type of situation described by the prophet Isaiah when he said that "every valley shall be exalted, and every mountain and hill shall be made low: and the crooked shall be made straight, and the rough places plain."[65]

The world will continue to experience a remarkable transformation in those days. Everything on the surface of the planet will be reorganized and changed. The land of Jerusalem in Palestine and the land of Zion in America "shall be turned back into their own place, and the earth shall be like as it was in the days before it was divided."[69] Then will come the thousand years in human history known as the Millennium, after which the earth itself will eventually die and be resurrected. All of this represents an important and miraculous sequence of events, part of a mortal probation, as it were, that the earth will accomplish in order to obtain its own type of salvation and exaltation.

It is prior to the Millennium, following a period of transformation and burning that will partially fill the measure of its creation, that the earth will commence the seventh thousand years and the final stage of its progression. On that occasion, prior to a death and resurrection, it will be restored to a more perfect and original condition and rewarded according to the principles and concepts of the Law of Restoration.

Such an unusual view of the earth, based on faith as well as intellect, is admittedly a very miraculous concept. It is different from geological and astronomical explanations and in some ways opposite. At the same time, the unorthodox aspects of the idea give it credibility when viewed within the context of biblical and Christian theology, and because of this, it relates particularly to the time period of the latter days and is an important part of the signs of the times!

Any sequence in regard to the signs of the times, especially those that pertain to the final part of the last days, is once again necessarily tentative and theoretical. Nevertheless, the implication is that sometime toward the end of this period, there will occur in the sky a miraculous phenomenon involving the sun, moon, and stars. This is a concept stating that the first two of these entities will be darkened someday and the third will fall from the sky. It is also a subject often spoken of in scripture but seldom understood. Indeed in very few places do we find a sign of the times that is more enigmatic and puzzling than this one. It is a concept vacillating between the factual and realistic, and the figurative or symbolic. But it is an important sign nonetheless and, in one way or another, will definitely happen.

The concept is introduced in the twenty-fourth chapter of Matthew when Jesus answers a question asked by his disciples. "What shall be the sign of thy coming," they said, "and of the end of the world?" Jesus informed them that certain events needed to occur before his second advent, including wars and rumors of wars, earthquakes in different places, famines, and pestilence. He also said that the gospel would first be preached throughout the world. It was then that he told them about the sun, moon, stars, and the sign of the Son of man.

"Immediately after the tribulation of those days shall the sun be darkened," he told them, "and the moon shall not give her light, and the stars shall fall from heaven, and the powers of the heavens shall be shaken: and then shall appear the sign of the Son of man in heaven: and then shall all the tribes of the earth mourn, and they shall see the Son of man coming in the clouds of heaven with power and great glory."[71]

In this preliminary report, the most surprising thing is undoubtedly the idea that stars would fall from heaven, certainly a remarkable statement. It was also mentioned that the sun would be darkened and the moon would refuse to give light. All of these are unusual occurrences, yet as far as the moon itself is concerned, nothing was ever said about it turning to blood as is stated in certain other scriptures.

The prophet Joel, for example, in talking about the signs in the sky, refers specifically to the moon turning to blood. "And I will shew wonders in the heavens and in the earth," he said, speaking for the Lord, "blood, and fire, and pillars of smoke. The sun shall be turned into darkness, and the moon into blood, before the great and the terrible day of the Lord come."[72]

Many times it is a matter of deciding whether or not the wording of scripture denotes a literal occurrence or one that is figurative or symbolic. And in the instances of stars falling out of the sky and the moon turning to blood, obviously a symbolic meaning is intended. Stars being planets, in other words, do not normally plummet through space like meteors, nor will the moon change into a different substance. Nevertheless, a particular prophet who occasionally makes such statements, and even the Lord on occasion, is effective in using this type of language, and his point is usually well taken.

The same is true in the book of Revelation in relation to the opening of the sixth seal where it says that "the sun became black as sackcloth of hair, and the moon became as blood."[73] Other references, such as those in the Doctrine and Covenants and the book of Joel, clearly state that the moon will be turned into blood.

"But, behold, I say unto you that before this great day shall come the sun shall be darkened, and the moon shall be turned into blood, and the stars shall fall from heaven, and there shall be greater signs in heaven above and in the earth beneath."[74]

Whatever the scriptural wording might be, the concept pertaining to the darkening or coloring of the sun and moon is interesting, and the type of language involved is usually understandable and acceptable. It is the statements referring to the stars that are particularly significant, not only concerning the stars themselves, but the constellations as well. In the book of Isaiah, for example, the prophet says that in the last days "the stars of heaven and the constellations thereof shall not give their light: the sun shall be darkened in his going forth, and the moon shall not cause her light to shine."[75]

The fact that Isaiah is the only prophet that refers to the constellations of the sky is noteworthy. And although he says nothing about them being in motion, only that they will refuse to give light, the idea is still important, suggesting that both they and the sun, moon, and stars will someday be perceived as performing in unexpected ways, consequently resulting in visual effects that will be important signs of the times.

A person needs only look at a map of the constellations in the two hemispheres to visualize what it would be like on future occasions when it appears that the constellations are moving or are in commotion. If only twelve of the constellations, for example, such as those which have given their names to the signs of the Zodiac, were observed at nighttime to be in some kind of disorder or confusion, along with their individual stars, it would naturally be a sign that something extremely important was about to take place, something that had never happened before. And indeed, just such a thing has been prophesied to occur in the future, namely that the stars in the heavens will be in disarray, showing that a countdown of certain critical events has begun and that the Second Coming is on its way!

In addition to the prophecy of Isaiah, there are other scriptures relating to the stars and to unusual language used in their description. It is some of the figurative expressions that are particularly interesting. The portrayal of stars becoming "exceedingly angry" and casting themselves down as recorded in Doctrine and Covenants 88:87, for example, illustrates the use of literary personification, as does their refusal to shine. Instances where it says that stars "fell unto the earth"[76] or were "hurled from their places"[77] also show an abnormal use of language as far as heavenly bodies are concerned. The different kinds of literary devices used by the prophets and authors of scripture are many.

"For not many days hence and the earth shall tremble and reel to and fro as a drunken man," the record says, as shown in the Doctrine and Covenants, "and the sun shall hide his face, and shall refuse to give light; and the moon shall be bathed in blood; and the stars shall become exceedingly angry, and shall cast themselves down as a fig that falleth from off a fig-tree."[78] In the book of Revelation there is similar wording which says that "the stars of heaven fell unto the earth, even as a fig tree casteth her untimely figs, when she is shaken of a mighty wind."[79]

In addition, there are those scriptures that suggest that the phenomenon of sun, moon, and stars will not only be a preliminary sign of the Lord's Second Coming, but also one relating to his Millennial reign on earth. "Then the moon shall be confounded," writes Isaiah, "and the sun ashamed, when the Lord of hosts shall reign in mount Zion, and in Jerusalem, and before his ancients gloriously."[80] Also in modern scripture in reference to the Lord, it says that "so great shall be the glory of his presence that the sun shall hide his face in shame, and the moon shall withhold its light, and the stars shall be hurled from their places."[81]

Again, the variety of references to the sun, moon, and stars constitutes a significant body of material, and it has prompted considerable comment and opinion among many who read and study the scriptures. Some regard the prophecies as events yet to come, whereas others are inclined to say that they have already been partially fulfilled. Because of pollutants in the air, for example, along with other factors pertaining to a modern technology, there have been times when the sun has been abnormally darkened, and certain chemicals in the air have sometimes given the moon an unusual reddish color. During violent earthquakes, which have been many, it might have seemed on occasion during nighttime that stars were falling or were in motion.

But impressive as phenomena such as these might be, they are still not the signs of the times that are mentioned in the scriptures. On the occasions of their occurrence, they have had a significant impact on those who have seen them, but these events undoubtedly have never reached the level of remarkableness, so to speak, which would equate them with what the Bible and other scriptures are talking about. Moreover, such things as a large volume of recorded UFO occurrences, regarded at times not only as abnormalities in the sky but as definite signs or omens, do not qualify.

It might rightfully be said, therefore, that when the sun is darkened in a scriptural sense, becoming "black as sackcloth of hair," and when the moon is reddened enough to be associated with blood, when an unusually large number of meteorites fall to the earth causing an untold amount of damage, only then can it be said that a most extraordinary event has happened for the first time and that a religious prophecy has been fulfilled. In other words, something much more than what modern technology can create, as sophisticated as it has become, will be needed to bring about a realization and fulfillment of the remarkable statements recorded in scripture.

The same might be said in connection with what is referred to as the sign of the Son of man, especially in regard to this particular sign. The only place where this scripture occurs in the Bible is in the twenty-fourth chapter of Matthew in the New Testament, yet it is enough to tentatively position it chronologically and differentiate it from other occurrences.

"Immediately after the tribulation of those days shall the sun be darkened," the scripture says, "and the moon shall not give her light, and the stars shall fall from heaven, and the powers of the heavens shall be shaken. And then shall appear the sign of the Son of man in heaven: and then shall the tribes of the earth mourn, and they shall see the Son of man coming in the clouds of heaven with power and great glory."[82] There is also a very brief scripture in the Doctrine and Covenants which states that all people shall see the sign together,[83] all of which poses the question as to what type of sign it will be and how it will differ from other phenomena in the sky.

Any answer to such a question, however, is elusive. The only clue is that it will follow soon after what happens to the sun, moon, and stars and will possibly be very close in time to the Second Coming itself. Some might claim to have seen it after witnessing an impressive display of comets or meteors, or other such phenomena, yet the implication of the prophecy is that this is an event that will be extraordinary and without precedent or parallel.

In reality, it could turn out to be a quiet, subtle event, more impressive because of its meaning and significance rather than any striking astronomic or stellar occurrence. But whatever it might be, and whenever it might occur, it will be one of the final signs of the times, a part of the last countdown of events that will eventually lead to the opening of heaven and the Second Coming of Christ!

As the final countdown of events draws closer to the last hour of time, the most reliable source of information, both as to time and sequence, is the record of scripture known as the Doctrine and Covenants. Only in this one source is there a brief account outlining the last and final events prior to the Second Coming.

"And he shall utter his voice out of Zion, and he shall speak from Jerusalem," the record states, referring to the Lord, "and his voice shall be heard among all people; and it shall be a voice as the voice of many waters, and as the voice of a great thunder, which shall break down the mountains, and the valleys shall not be found. He shall command the great deep, and it shall be driven back into the north countries, and the islands shall become one land; and the land of Jerusalem and the land of Zion shall be turned back into their own place, and the earth shall be like as it was in the days before it was divided."[84]

This particular scripture describes important events and circumstances occurring a short time before the beginning of the Millennium, namely those leading up to the inevitable climax known as the end of the world. The sequence of things is not entirely clear, yet there is an implication that a definite sequence does exist. In connection with the massive string of earthquakes, for example, it is logical that a transformation and restructuring of the earth's surface will take place during that specific period of time. This is when mountains will fall all across the planet, and the topography of the earth's surface will become increasingly level and more like a plain.

Then at a later time, following the phenomena in the sky relating to the sun, moon, and stars, the waters of the great deep will be driven back into the north country, and the earth's land surface will be transformed into a single continent adjoining a much smaller surface of water. And although the scripture in the Doctrine and Covenants at first might suggest that a transformation of land occurs *after* the water action, logic once again would say that it will happen *before*, at the time of the earthquakes! First comes the geologic change, and then the hydraulic.

In any case, this event brings the world toward the end of the last countdown. At a time in history when a tremendous shaking of the planet has resulted in a restructuring and transformation of the earth's land surface, and after the phenomenon relating to the sun, moon, and stars has taken place, as well as the sign of the Son of man, it is that time also when a huge volume of sea and ocean will recede into the north country to be driven, as it were, to a new location. On that occasion, the areas of Jerusalem and Palestine in the east and the city and land of Zion in the west will "be turned back into their own place," the result of a recession of water in some ways as well as geologic transformation, and the earth will become like it was in the days before it was divided.

Certainly these will be remarkable and miraculous events, including the one pertaining to water. To visualize a large part of the Pacific and Atlantic Oceans, along with their adjacent seas, all referred to scripturally as the "waters of the great deep,"[85] relocating someday to the north and at the same time logically resulting in a much lower sea level is very difficult to understand without knowing some kind of meaningful reason or purpose. Merely to say that a huge volume of water will turn northward without any place to go when it gets there does not hold with reality. Consequently, there has to be some kind of explanation and, as it turns out, it is found not only in the statement in the Doctrine and Covenants that talks about the earth and the time before it was divided but also in the reference to the division of the earth mentioned in the book of Genesis.

In the tenth chapter of Genesis in the twenty-fifth verse, an unusual and controversial scripture is recorded. "And unto Eber were born two sons: the name of one was Peleg; for in his days was the earth divided; and his brother's name was Joktan."

That is all that is said about it. There is no further information given. It is as though a sudden thought were suddenly sandwiched between two relatively unimportant items of genealogy for some unknown purpose. Consequently, the scripture has generated considerable conjecture and speculation for many years as to what is actually meant by a division of the earth.

What kind of division was the ancient prophet and historian of Genesis talking about when he said that the earth was divided? What purpose did it serve to introduce this kind of topic so dramatically and unexpectedly? Regarding these questions, many answers have been given, with historians and biblical scholars differing so widely that any consensus of opinion appears unlikely. Yet there is possibly a correct answer, one which explains the mysterious recession of seas and oceans into the north country, at the same time giving important scriptural evidence and information that provide an interesting adjunct to the provocative signs of the times!

Several meanings have been given to the statement that the earth was divided in the days of Peleg. All of these relate in one way or another to the etymology of Peleg's name, which in the Hebrew language signifies *watercourse* and *division.* Whatever it was that happened in those days, it was an important event, enough so that Peleg was named after it. The scripture in the first book of Chronicles, almost identical to the one in Genesis except for the word *because,* states very clearly the reason for such a name. "And unto Eber were born two sons: the name of the one was Peleg; because in his days the earth was divided: and his brother's name was Joktan."[86]

The important question, of course, is what is meant by the word *divided.* What happened in ancient times to prompt such an unusual term or expression? Moreover, was the event something that should be considered literally, or just figuratively and symbolically, and how might it relate to a tremendous volume of water being driven to the northern part of the globe? Such a brief reference in scripture obviously creates a problem, as well as a question, and consequently, there are at least eleven different explanations or theories which present a possible solution.

(1) The most prominent theory, and the one most prevalent in the literature, is that *divided* refers to a division of people.

This meaning is suggested early in the tenth chapter of Genesis, just prior to the account of Peleg and Joktan's birth. Referring to the descendants of Japhath, the son of Noah, the scripture reads as follows: "By these were the isles of the Gentiles divided in their lands; every one after his tongue, after their families, in their nations."[87]

Only a few verses following the passage in connection with Peleg, the word *divided* is again used in the same way. "These are the families of the sons of Noah," the scripture states, "after their generations, in their nations: and by these were the nations divided in the earth after the flood."[88]

Any normal reading of Genesis in regard to these passages would likely result in one conclusion, namely that the division of the earth in the days of Peleg pertained to a division of people, both linguistically and geographically. Especially with *divided* being used three times in fairly rapid succession, the implication is that in all three instances, the same kind event is involved, namely a separation and scattering of the population with the confusion of tongues at the Tower of Babel being a principal factor.

(2) Another interpretation of the word in question is that it refers to the time when Peleg and Joktan separated and went their different ways. When the latter left his homeland to migrate southward into the Arabian Peninsula, for example, he took his thirteen sons with him, and there they became the leaders of thirteen different tribes. Peleg, in the meantime, apparently remained in the Mesopotamian area, with the result being that a significant division occurred among the people, more specifically within the family of Eber.

Since Eber is traditionally considered to be the progenitor of the Hebrews, the separation of his two sons who are mentioned by name in the Bible certainly could be interpreted as a dividing point, Peleg continuing on in the patriarchal line and Joktan establishing a well-known ethnic group called Joktanide Arabs. Like Isaac and Ishmael later on, and also Jacob and Esau, these two brothers represented important milestones in history, each playing a vital part in the development of nations in the area of the Middle East.

(3) A third explanation of the word *divided* pertains to a political and geographical division of territory. It might have involved the establishment of certain types of territorial limits or municipal boundaries, but whatever it was, if it actually happened during Peleg's time, it evidently had an important impact on a large population of people.

(4) In contrast to these theories, there is also the idea that the division of the earth referred more accurately to irrigation and agriculture. The etymology of Peleg's name, in fact, has to do with water as well as division. Associated with the origin of the word are such meanings as *watercourse, canal,* and *channel.* In those early days, the earth might have been thought of as being divided when people in Mesopotamia started building extensive irrigation canals.

Peleg's birth may have coincided with agricultural inventions that were significant enough to warrant his family giving him a special name. Certainly few things were more important than water at that time, and when irrigation canals began crisscrossing the countryside, where earlier there had been only unproductive land, it naturally could have been regarded as a unique event, enough so that more persons than one might have been given the name of Peleg.

(5) Another meaning of *divided* is that it was the conclusion of the great flood during the time of Noah. Instead of water rapidly draining off from the earth, as recorded in the Bible, it is suggested that it subsided much more slowly, not stopping until the days of Peleg, at which time the division of land into islands and continents finally became complete.

(6) Along with these explanations, some minor ones also exist, including (a) a mystical interpretation pertaining to the separation of the sexes, (b) the point in the development of man when he realized that his material or physical nature was separate from his inner spiritual self, (c) a separation of mankind

into different groups because of quarrels and dissensions, even before the Tower of Babel, and (d) a dividing point in history when people's life spans became significantly shortened.

(7) Then finally, there are still two other theories which relate to a division of the earth, both relatively minor as far as their prevalence in the literature is concerned. Yet one of them could possibly be the explanation that comes closer to the truth. The first refers to a breakup in the earth's original landmass as described in the theory of continental drift, while the other involves a gigantic deluge of water, a second but smaller flood, as it were, in relatively close succession to the one before it, which inundated large sections of land and created the present-day islands and continents.

Both of these views, characterized by highly physical phenomena, differ markedly with most of the other explanations, as well as with one another. Each presents a very different idea as to what happened when the earth's land surface was divided in the days of Peleg. Yet when everything is considered, one of them shows a definite advantage over the other, especially in regard to chronology and certain principles of modern-day science!

The theory of continental drift states that the lower half of Africa's west coast at one time adjoined the eastern coast of South America and that the rest of Africa connected mainly with the eastern part of North America. Other sections of the earth joined together in a similar way, all forming one landmass. Then came a time when the land started drifting apart to form continents, continuing to do so until it arrived at the condition in which it appears today. This theory at present is generally a well-accepted concept and is referred to in the scientific community as *plate tectonics*.

There is a time problem, however, in associating the drifting continents with what took place during the days of Peleg. Scientists estimate that landforms started moving sometime between two hundred and three hundred million years ago, whereas Bible chronologists place Peleg's time at about 2250 BC, or according to a different chronology, several centuries earlier.

Of course it could be said that in this instance, due to divine intervention, things happened much more quickly. There are those places in scripture, for example, which suggest that rapid changes in geology sometimes occur but are later attributed to long passages of time.

It could also be said that science has been wrong before, and in this case it could be wrong again. And yet in regard to this particular situation, it probably would be well to avoid conflict between an important biblical event and a popular scientific idea. Besides, another explanation and one that is much more applicable to the time of Peleg definitely exists.

This last theory is one that is supported by both ancient and modern scripture and at the same time more acceptable in terms of science. It is the idea of water coming in upon the earth via rainfall and underground sources, especially the latter, inundating large areas of land and causing a mammoth division of territory. It was very similar to what happened during the great flood, except the incoming water was now far less extensive. Whereas complete inundation allegedly occurred in the first instance, only a partial one took place in the second.

It was also a deluge that was separate and distinct from the one before it. Although the idea of two major floods occurring so close to one another might at first seem improbable, there are reasons for believing that such a thing actually did happen.

In comparison with continental drift, this kind of explanation is much more likely to avoid an unnecessary confrontation between scientific theory and the Bible, as well as present a logical view of what might have taken place. It is also an idea which is more tenable as far as the etymology of Peleg's name is concerned. And the one main clue in reaching these conclusions is found in a very unexpected place, hidden in a remote and secluded location in scripture! Very brief in content, it occurs suddenly and unexpectedly, much like its companion material in the Bible.

There are only two verses of biblical scripture, one in Genesis and the other in the book of First Chronicles, that mention the division of the earth during the days of Peleg. Extremely brief and ambiguous, they have long been a puzzle to biblical scholars and have often resulted in significant problems. Ironically, there is the same number of verses in the Doctrine and Covenants, just as brief in wording and content, that refer to this same event. And it is this last piece of information that finally unravels the mystery of what the account in the Bible pertaining to a division actually means.

Besides explaining the word *divided* itself, relating it specifically to a large deluge of water, these two verses of scripture also establish the cause of the deluge, as well as its geographical source!

Referring to the latter days and the Second Coming of Jesus Christ, the verses read as follows: "He shall command the great deep, and it shall be driven back into the north countries, and the islands shall become one land; And the land of Jerusalem and the land of Zion shall be turned back into their own place, and the earth shall be like as it was in the days before it was divided."[89]

This one scripture, providing valuable information and insight, answers several puzzling questions. First, the division of the earth during Peleg's time was the result of incoming water, an extreme flooding of the land which created the outline and perimeter of hundreds of islands and seven continents.

Second, the statement that the water "shall be driven back into the north countries"[89] is a strong implication that this is where it came from in the first place, originating somewhere in the northern part of the globe, apparently in places of outlet permitting the effluence of huge amounts of subterranean water. It came down from the north, in other words, and it will someday go back to the north. Within the context of this scripture, water "gathered together unto one place," as described in the biblical account of the Creation, takes on a different kind of significance, or at least a double meaning and second interpretation.

Third, it is especially important, after the many opinions that have been given, to learn more about the word *divided* as it is used in the books of Genesis and First Chronicles. To some it might seem like a small thing, but for others it stands as a unique and outstanding discovery. There appears to be considerable evidence now that the term in question refers to a remarkable deluge during the days of

Peleg, reminiscent also of the time of Creation and the great flood in the days of Noah!

It is ironic, however, that so little is said in scripture concerning such momentous events as the division of the earth and a return of floodwaters to the north country. Aside from the references in Genesis, First Chronicles, and the Doctrine and Covenants, all of which are brief, only two other scriptures talk about this division, both occurring in the book of Revelation.

The scripture in Revelation 6:14, for example, where multiple meanings are involved, reads as follows: "And the heaven departed as a scroll when it is rolled together; and every mountain and island were moved out of their places." In this instance, it is possible that a reference to mountains might refer to their destruction as a result of quaking and breakdown, but viewing mountains and islands together, both moving out of their places, a more likely interpretation is that their change of situation would be due to the recession of surrounding water.

The scripture in Revelation 16:20 conveys essentially the same meaning when it says that "every island fled away, and the mountains were not found." The idea once again is that mountains and islands will not geologically be dismantled and removed, but their geographical and topographical situation will change because of the recession of the great deep and a mammoth decrease in water.

Finally, there is the question of where water will go after it is driven into the north countries, a question which at present has no definite answer. All that can be said is that it remains one of the mysteries of this particular area of the globe. Yet there are theories and speculation that somewhere in the far north, the earth has the hydraulic capacity to emit and absorb enormous quantities of subterranean water. With what happened at the time of the Creation and in the days of Noah serving as a precedent, the phenomenon of water emerging onto the earth during the time of Peleg definitely approaches reality, a situation in which the water involved will someday be driven back again to the north where it first appeared.

Theoretically this means that three times during the world's history, water has emerged from subterranean reservoirs and covered all or part of the earth's surface. Twice it has receded and returned to its original location. And once again at a time during the latter days, shortly before the Second Coming of Jesus Christ, it will recede one last time as the waters of the great deep respond to a divine command and are driven back into the north countries!

The wording in the Doctrine and Covenants saying that water will be driven back is unconventional and interesting. The meaning of the language solicits a variety of opinions. One idea, for example, referring to water moving to the north, is that there will be a thunderous noise as an entire ocean relocates, associating the account with that in an adjoining scripture that refers to "the voice of many waters."

This kind of action, however, is possibly too dramatic, a more plausible occurrence being that the receding water will follow more closely what took place when waters were gathered together during the Creation and after the great flood. On those occasions, at least in Noah's time, it took five or five and one-half months for floodwaters to recede, and a similar amount of time might be involved when the water originating during the time of Peleg recedes into the north countries.

This means that in the future, after the surface of the earth has been restructured and transformed by way of earthquakes, further changes will take place via the eroding and sculpting effects of water as it returns to its original source, everything being prepared for an eventual burning and cleansing at the end of the world. Simultaneously, people will continue the process of everyday living, observing the many changes taking place during an undetermined period of time. Following the Battle of Armageddon, for example, it will take seven months to bury the dead, according to the Bible, and seven years to burn the weapons of war and refuse. Many other things will also be taking place. The concluding events and circumstances during this time period will undoubtedly be varied and unusual, but everything will continue as in the past. Prior to the time of the Second Coming, people most likely will be doing what they have always done, and then one day, suddenly and unexpectedly, the end will come!

But in the meantime, there is still one concluding question, one that relates to the time when the earth was divided in the days of Peleg. It asks once more why so little has been said about this important event. Why is it that scripture mentions it only briefly and with little or no explanation? And why is there nothing said about it in secular history?

Again, it is one of those times when apparently no one knows of an answer, and any final resolution of things is evidently reserved for the future. But there is a theory once again, one related to the idea that not too long after the flood in the time of Noah, water again came down out of the north country, inundating large areas of land and dividing the earth in the days of Peleg. In commemoration of the event, because he was born generally at the same time, Peleg was given his unusual name.

This was only one hundred years after the flood, according to the chronology of sources such as the King James Version of the Bible, and most people had not had enough time yet to travel great distances in any direction. Consequently, the majority was most likely unaware that any extensive flooding had occurred and that the so-called division had taken place, the result being that very little was ever said or written about it. It is probable that only a very few knew what was happening at the time, among them being those involved in the naming of Peleg. As things turned out, it was that time in history when the world's population was drastically diminished as a result of the great flood, and because of it, the idea of a division never had a chance to materialize.

But allegedly, the division in the days of Peleg did occur, and the new waterways among seven continents and countless islands became highways, as it were, for future migration and colonization. At that time, the world was on the verge of a new era of discovery and at the threshold of destiny and fortune which lay ahead. It was a new world of adventure and opportunity. And inevitably on the distant horizon, as men and ships now crossed the new seas and oceans, there were also those future events pending and waiting that ultimately would lead to the end of human affairs on a telestial earth and provide a gateway to the Millennium!

At the conclusion of six remarkable events, some of them almost unbelievable in their conditions and circumstances, the final step in the last countdown now begins! The crowning event and climax before the Second Coming, and the most important occurrence in history since the meridian of time, finally commences! All of the events in the countdown so far are merely a prelude to what now takes place.

At a prescribed time, which Jesus on one occasion said was known only to his Father, the curtain of heaven will suddenly be raised and unfolded! In a manner unidentified and unexplained, the covering obstructing a view of heaven will be removed, and the Lord's presence will be revealed. Certainly it is difficult to describe what will actually happen at this time, and the few scriptures relating to it at first seem ambiguous and confusing. Indeed a description of this particular event in the book of Revelation has been referred to as a very difficult expression. It is especially difficult when associated with a scroll. "And the heaven departed," the scripture says, "as a scroll when it is rolled together."[90]

An initial reading of this verse presents a picture of heaven leaving, much like a written scroll disappearing from view when it is rolled up. Again, it is a very difficult image to visualize and a hard one to understand, and because of this, there are undoubtedly many opinions.

The correct image, however, is one that is in direct opposition to a scroll being rolled up, rather one where it is opened or undone, *after* it has been rolled together. Instead of the sky being viewed symbolically as a pliant or flexible expanse which can be rolled together, the meaning in the scripture is that the heavens will be *opened*. Joseph Smith was of this opinion also when he interpreted Revelation 6:14, saying, "And the heavens opened as a scroll is opened when it is rolled together."[91]

The meaning of this type of wording is further complicated by its use in the book of Isaiah where the prophet writes, "And all the host of heaven shall be dissolved, and the heavens shall be rolled together as a scroll."[92] And although the wording here is similar, it apparently has a very different interpretation, one relating to the dissolution of the heavens and the creation of new heavens and a new earth.

Finally, it is in another record, the Doctrine and Covenants, where clear and unmistakable language depicts what will actually occur in regard to the curtain of heaven. In brief but certain terms, the vocabulary and phrasing in the book of Revelation are paraphrased and explained.

"And there shall be silence in heaven for the space of half an hour; and immediately after shall the curtain of heaven be unfolded, as a scroll is unfolded after it is rolled up, and the face of the Lord shall be unveiled."[93]

The point in all of this, of course, is that this is the exact moment in history when the Second Coming occurs, the calendar date also for the approach of the biblical Millennium. This is not the time of the giant holocaust and burning which will later take place on the earth's surface, but rather the resplendent time of resurrection that precedes it. It is only after the latter has happened that the worldwide burning of the planet will occur.

Surely this will be a time of celebration for those who have led righteous lives, yet at the same time, one of mourning and remorse for those who have done otherwise. It is that time in world history when the clock stops, as it were, and the Lord makes his first official appearance among the people, a time when all of the righteous, both the living and the dead, are called up to meet him in the clouds of glory.

Then according to the right time and sequence, at a time designated as the end of the world, the earth will finally be burned and cleansed, after which a second genesis will occur and also a brand new beginning, one with an entirely new social order, as well as one that is political, and mankind for the first time will know what it is like to be in the Millennium!

THE QUESTION OF THE SEVENTH SEAL

A reference to the curtain of heaven once more raises
the question of why such a phenomenon occurs in the book
of Revelation in connection with the sixth seal instead of
the seventh. Is this how the author of the book recorded it
initially, or has something happened in the meantime to alter
the meaning?

There appears to be no explanation at present why an event
obviously belonging to the seventh seal, namely the unfolding
of the curtain of heaven, should be listed as part of the sixth.
The same is true regarding the moving of mountains and
islands out of their places, and possibly two other events as
well: the great earthquake and the sky phenomenon.

Obvious problems do exist, therefore, and their resolution
again is evidently one that is reserved for the future. At some
undetermined time, there will eventually come an answer.
In the meantime, there will always be a second question, a
probing one as to when the seventh millennium begins, if it has
not already begun. In other words, when will revelation and
prophecy be fulfilled concerning the seventh thousand years?
The scripture states that in the beginning of that period, the
Lord will complete the salvation of man, during which time
he will prepare and finish his work, "the preparing of the way
before the time of his coming."[94]

A look at the calendar, if chronology is close to being correct, definitely gives the impression that today is the time, the present moment when things materialize and begin taking place. Surely it is evident that current events and circumstances give the idea that world society is rapidly nearing some kind of countdown. A sudden increase in temple building by The Church of Jesus Christ of Latter-day Saints during the last twenty years, for example, presages the future construction of temples in both western Missouri and Jerusalem. In the meantime, as the signs begin to appear, people everywhere remain complacent or unaware of any kind of return of ten lost tribes. There is also an increased awareness and concern regarding earthquakes, as well as oceans going beyond their bounds, while an increasing resentment and antagonism toward Israel bespeaks more and more of Armageddon.

Certainly, these are significant signs of the times and a forecast of many possibilities for the future. Very possibly also, they represent a time period that is already beyond the opening of the seventh seal and the beginning of the seventh millennium. Yet whenever the final situations do occur, if indeed some of them are not already well underway, the ultimate destiny of the future still lies just ahead and will take place on schedule at the time of the Second Coming!

Among the infinite possible numbers that exist, the number seven is possibly the most interesting and significant. The seven days of the week always serve as a reminder of this. But it is in the pages of the Bible that the number takes on additional importance and meaning. It was during six creative periods, for example, that God made the heavens and the earth, after which, during the seventh, he celebrated the occasion by making it a day of rest. Since that time, the Sabbath and the number seven have both become important symbols.

"And on the seventh day God ended his work which he had made; and he rested on the seventh day from all his work . . . And God blessed the seventh day, and sanctified it."[95]

It is true that certain numbers in the Bible have acquired symbolic meaning in addition to designating quantity. Besides seven, there is important symbolism in such numbers as twelve, three, four, and forty. But undoubtedly it is seven that is the most well-known and significant.

In many instances in scripture, the number has come to represent three main ideas: perfection, fulfillment, and completeness. This is apparent in regard to the time of the Creation, but it also relates to the statement that the earth at present is going through a period of temporal existence amounting to seven thousand years. There is also a scriptural reference to seven angels with trumpets announcing some of the important events pertaining to the beginning of the seventh millennium, those preparing the way for the Second Coming.

In addition to angels with trumpets, there are also those mentioned in the Bible who carry seven golden vials containing the seven last plagues. Indeed, there are many places in both the Old and New Testaments where the number seven is an important factor.

It is seven events during the last days, however, beginning with the return of the lost tribes of Israel, that are particularly significant. Purported to be the occurrences and circumstances immediately preceding the Second Coming of Jesus Christ, they are to be instrumental in preparing the earth for the coming Millennium. Unquestionably, they will be among the latter-day occurrences which will enable the earth to finally achieve its destiny, one having to do with completeness and fulfillment, as well as paradisiacal glory and perfection. Indeed, these are the seven events that will constitute the consummation and grand denouement of human affairs at the end of the world's regular history, the inevitable climax and dramatic conclusion of the final countdown!

REFERENCES

Note: The King James Version of the Bible, the Book of Mormon, and the Doctrine and Covenants are standard works of The Church of Jesus Christ of Latter-day Saints.

1. Revelation 6–8.
2. Doctrine and Covenants 77:6.
3. Doctrine and Covenants 77:12.
4. Revelation 6:9.
5. Revelation 6:12–14.
6. Revelation 8:2.
7. Doctrine and Covenants 77:12.
8. Isaiah 2:3.
9. Ezekiel 40.
10. Joseph Smith Jr., *History of The Church of Jesus Christ of Latter-day Saints*, ed. B. H. Roberts, rev. ed. (Salt Lake City: Deseret Book, 1951), 5:337.
11. Doctrine and Covenants 84:4.
12. Doctrine and Covenants 84:2.
13. Doctrine and Covenants 115:6.
14. Doctrine and Covenants 88:19.
15. Ephesians 1:10.
16. Joseph Smith Jr., *History of The Church of Jesus Christ of Latter-day Saints*, ed. B. H. Roberts, rev. ed. (Salt Lake City: Deseret Book Company, 1951), 4:211–212.
17. The Temple Institute. http://www.templeinstitute.org/main.htm.
18. Karen Boren Swedin, "Jews and Moslems—Both Bitter Enemies—Consider Temple Mount as Hold Ground," Deseret News, October 14,1990.
19. Joseph Smith Jr., *History of the Church of Jesus Christ of Latter-Day Saints*, ed. B. H. Roberts, rev. ed. (Salt Lake City: Deseret Book, 1951), 5:337.
20. Ezekiel 47:1, 8–9.

21. Joel 3:18.

22. Zechariah 14:8.

23. Doctrine and Covenants 107:53–56.

24. Doctrine and Covenants 116 and 117:8.

25. Daniel 7:9–10.

26. Daniel 7:13–14.

27. Joseph Smith Jr., *History of The Church of Jesus Christ of Latter-day Saints*, ed. B. H. Roberts., rev. ed. (Salt Lake City: Deseret Book), 3:386–387.

28. Daniel 7:15, 28.

29. Revelation 8:3–6.

30. Doctrine 77:12.

31. Revelation 8:12.

32. Joseph Smith Jr., *History of The Church of Jesus Christ of Latter-day Saints*, ed. B. H. Roberts., rev. ed. (Salt Lake City: Deseret Book), 1:439–440.

33. Ibid., 440.

34. Joel 2:30.

35. Luke 21:25.

36. Baron Max Von Oppenheim, *Tell Halaf* (Piscataway, NJ: Gorgias Press, 2006), p.39.

37. Bruce M. Metzger, ed., *The Apocrypha of the Old Testament*, Revised Standard Version (New York: Oxford University Press, 1965), p. 65.

38. Doctrine and Covenants 91:1–2.

39. Bruce M. Metzger, ed., *The Apocrypha of the Old Testament*, Revised Standard Version (New York: Oxford University Press, 1965), p. 65.

40. Amos 9:9.

41. R. Clayton Brough, *The Lost Tribes* (Salt Lake City: Horizon Publishers, 1979), p. 44.

42. Doctrine and Covenants 133:26–34.

43. Bruce M. Metzger, ed., *The Apocrypha of the Old Testament*, Revised Standard Version (New York: Oxford University Press, 1965), p. 65.

44. James E. Talmage, *Conference Report of The Church of*

Jesus Christ of Latter-day Saints, April 1916, p. 13.

45. Revelation 16:14,16.
46. Ezekiel 38:2.
47. Joel 2:2.
48. Ezekiel 38:15.
49. Ezekiel 38:4.
50. Joel 2:2–3.
51. Revelation 16:18.
52. Zechariah 14:5.
53. Revelation 19:17.
54. Ezekiel 39:17–20.
55. Ezekiel 39:9–13.
56. Doctrine and Covenants 45:48.
57. Doctrine and Covenants 88:88–91.
58. Revelation 11:13.
59. Revelation 16:18–19.
60. Zechariah 14:2.
61. Luke 21:24.
62. Ezekiel 38:19–20.
63. Haggai 2:6–7.
64. Isaiah 24:18–20.
65. Isaiah 40:4–5.
66. Luke 3:5–6.
67. Doctrine and Covenants 49:23.
68. Doctrine and Covenants 88:87.
69. Doctrine and Covenants 133:21–22, 24.
70. Acts 3:20–21.
71. Matthew 24:29–30.
72. Joel 2:30–31.
73. Revelation 6:12.
74. Doctrine and Covenants 29:14.
75. Isaiah 13:10.
76. Revelation 6:13.
77. Doctrine and Covenants 133:49.
78. Doctrine and Covenants 88:87.
79. Revelation 6:13.

80. Isaiah 24:23.

81. Doctrine and Covenants 133:49.

82. Matthew 24:29–30.

83. Doctrine and Covenants 88:93.

84. Doctrine and Covenants 133:21–24.

85. Isaiah 51:10.

86. I Chronicles 1:19.

87. Genesis 10:5.

88. Genesis 10:32.

89. Doctrine and Covenants 133:23–24.

90. Revelation 6:14.

91. JST Revelation 6:14.

92. Isaiah 34:4.

93. Doctrine and Covenants 88:95.

94. Doctrine and Covenants 77:12.

95. Genesis 2:2–3.

Clay McConkie is a native of Utah. He is a teacher by occupation, having taught in Salt Lake City schools for thirty years. He received a BA from Brigham Young University and an MS and PhD from the University of Utah. He and his wife reside in Provo, Utah, and are the parents of four children.

He is also the author of *One Flesh, The Gathering of the Waters, The Ten Lost Tribes, In Ephraim's Footsteps, In His Father's Image,* and *600 BC.*